The Poetry Review

The Poetry Society, 22 Betterton Street, London WC2H 9BX

The Poetry Review

The Poetry Society, 22 Betterton Street, London WC2H 9BX
Tel: +44 (0)20 7420 9880 • Fax: +44 (0)20 7240 4818
Email: poetryreview@poetrysociety.org.uk
poetrysociety.org.uk/thepoetryreview

Editor: Emily Berry
Production: Michael Sims

ISBN: 978-1-900771-31-8 ISSN: 0032 2156
Cover artwork: Kate Dehler, katedehler.com
Cover quote by Philip Gross, see p. 15

© The Poetry Review & The Poetry Society, 2021

. . .

SUBMISSIONS
We welcome submissions. Guidelines available
at poetrysociety.org.uk/thepoetryreview

ADVERTISING
To advertise in *The Poetry Review*, visit
poetrysociety.org.uk/thepoetryreview or
contact Ben Rogers on +44 (0)20 7420 9880,
email: marketing@poetrysociety.org.uk

BOOKSHOP DISTRIBUTION
Central Books, 50 Freshwater Road, London
RM8 1RX, UK. Tel: +44 (0)20 8525 8800
or visit centralbooks.com

PBS OFFER TO POETRY SOCIETY MEMBERS
The Poetry Book Society offers Poetry Society
Members a special 10% discount (plus postage)
on books bought from poetrybooks.co.uk.
Contact The Poetry Society: +44 (0)20 7420
9880 or membership@poetrysociety.org.uk

SUBSCRIPTIONS & SALES
Individuals UK: £38 / Europe: £48
Rest of the World: £53 (delivery by airmail)
Single issue: £9.50 plus postage.
Order online at poetrysociety.org.uk/shop

Subscribe to the digital archive of *The Poetry
Review* at exacteditions.com/thepoetryreview
The Poetry Review is on sale in leading
bookshops. It is also available on audio CD.

The Poetry Review is the magazine of
The Poetry Society and was first published in
1912. A subscription to *The Poetry Review* is
included as part of membership of The Poetry
Society. Views expressed in *The Poetry Review*
are not necessarily those of The Poetry Society;
those of individual contributors are not
necessarily those of the Editor.

Charity Commission No. 303334.

*The Forest Stewardship Council (FSC) promotes environmentally appropriate, socially beneficial,
and economically viable management of the world's forests. By buying products with an FSC label you
are supporting the growth of responsible forest management worldwide. The Poetry Review is printed
with vegetable-based inks. Surplus inks, plates and printing blankets are recycled.*

THEPOETRYSOCIETY

CONTENTS

Poems

Amy Roa	Song	7
Shane McCrae	Explaining My Appearance in Certain Pictures	8
	Far Past the End	
	The Fungus Called Dead Man's Fingers	
	The Dead Negro in the Modernist Long Poem	
Philip Gross	Early Nocturne, Penarth Head	14
	The Named Storm	
Kathryn Maris	Because I too feel the violence of ▇▇▇	16
	I do not insert myself into conflicts	
	Echopoem	
Melissanthi / Kathryn Maris	Narcissus	19
Rachael Allen	*from* God Complex	20
Goliarda Sapienza / Brian Robert Moore	*from* Ancestral	25
Yvonne Reddick	Esther in the Asylum Garden	27
Ian Duhig	Tine	28
	Pheasant's Eye	
	An Arbitrary Light Bulb	
Tim Liardet	When I Hear Mr Blum, the Funeral Director,	31
Karen McCarthy Woolf	*from* un/safe	32
Sylvia Legris	Pomegranate, Carthaginian Apple	38
	Hare	
	Sheathfish [sic]	
	Earthworm	
	Map of Medical Materials	
	Topography of Repeating Plants and Patterns	

Essays

Listening for Stars: Mina Gorji on Coleridge, Oswald, Wordsworth   44
and Hadfield

Poems

Edward Doegar	*from* I never thought it would come to this	56
Nyla Matuk	On Palaces	59
Krisztina Tóth / Owen Good	Time, Time, Time	61
Sarala Estruch	Ghazal: Say denial (i)	63
K Patrick	Pickup truck sex Walk	65
Colin Channer	Lent	67
Sheri Benning	Of Ponteix, Saskatchewan: July 1929 If she did not	71
Taylor Strickland	Lichen Heil Valley	76
Polly Atkin	Mast Year / Helplessness Subscale Gravitas / Rumination Subscale	78
'Gbenga Adeoba	Tableau 20 Gbogi Street (Revisited)	80

Essays

On the Bone: Natalya Anderson on Twyla Tharp and Sharon Olds	82
Of Many Voices: A Poetic Gift of Togetherness by Karen Simecek, with a poem by Momtaza Mehri	92

Reviews

Stephanie Burt reviews Jack Underwood's non-fiction	101
Declan Ryan on John Burnside and Nuzhat Bukhari	106
Clare Pollard reviews a new *Selected Poems* by Wanda Coleman	110
Naush Sabah on a new reading of Keats's odes	115
Katrina Naomi on Abeer Ameer, Dom Bury and Victoria Kennefick	120
Stephanie Sy-Quia reviews alice hiller and Penelope Shuttle	125
Mantra Mukim on Jason Allen-Paisant and Ralf Webb	130
James Byrne reviews Fred D'Aguiar and Yousif M. Qasmiyeh	135
Lucy Mercer on Joyelle McSweeney	141

EDITORIAL

"I am so afraid of the words of men. / They pronounce everything so distinctly", Rilke wrote in an early poem ('Ich fürchte mich so vor der Menschen Wort', translator unknown). In these pages, reviewer Mantra Mukim briefly touches on this ambivalence of Rilke's about naming in his discussion of Jason Allen-Paisant's *Thinking with Trees*, an aside that sent me off down this rabbit-hole. "And this is called dog and that is called house," the poem continues, "And here is the beginning and the end is there. [...] // I shall always warn and ward off: Don't come near." Rilke was attracted to the *Namenlos*, nameless, a word that recurs in his work – he preferred the hole to the rabbits. His feeling about the nameless seems to stand in contrast to Audre Lorde's famous remark in 'Poetry Is Not a Luxury' that "Poetry is the way we help give name to the nameless so it can be thought". Yet she did write "*help* give name", as though to imply that naming is a force unto itself, and poets only midwives. However we feel about naming, we keep on doing it. "is it innate", Karen McCarthy Woolf writes in her sequence *un/safe*, "the urge / to fill that which / appears / to be / empty ?"

Philip Gross's 'The Named Storm' wonders whether to name is also to invoke and if so what we might be summoning – what forces a storm might accrue through its naming. "Could this have been our doing: we had called her / by name?" As so often I go back to Mary Ruefle's lecture 'On Secrets', in which, among other things, she warns us about names: "There is simply too much power in certain words, and the unnerving force of naming casts a great spell over language". If naming something breathes life into it, it also begets destruction, since a name can never contain all it claims to encompass: "because there is in this world no one thing / to which the bramble of *blackberry* corresponds, / a word is elegy to what it signifies", as Robert Hass put it in 'Meditation at Lagunitas'. To be given life is to be made mortal, as Lucy Mercer points out in her review of Joyelle McSweeney's *Toxicon & Arachne*: "to have a child is also always to bring a death into the world, to excavate a grave in the future."

In Allen-Paisant's poem 'Naming', discussed in Mukim's review, the speaker starts off wishing for a precision of language that Rilke rejects – he wants to know "the names of birds" and "identify them by their song", "because / a name is / reassurance" in a landscape where he does not feel at home. But he ends up in a similar place to Rilke, concluding that "perhaps the place within / will always escape the name". Maybe all poetry arises from this negotiation between the nameless and the urge to name, from the tension between them that never slackens: the nameless will "always escape", its getaway guaranteed in the very act of naming – just like the "named storm", whose "absence [is] still more *here* for being named".

We say release, and radiance, and roses,
and echo upon everything that's known,
and yet, behind the world our names enclose is
the nameless: our true archetype and home.
– Rilke, tr. Stephen Mitchell

Emily Berry

AMY ROA

Song

"What's the source of all sound?"
the man with a parasitic twin brother on his chest asked the man with a
   bouquet of flowers for a head.
They looked strong, and everything they knew they learned from the horseflies
   and wild boars they kept hidden in the basement.
I wish I could say I dove under the table when I heard chronicles of their wars,
   but I laughed loudly and hissed.
The effects of a childhood disease left untreated, I explained.
The twin on the brother's chest kicked back the remains of his beer.
He said, "The way I see it, one side of the brain controls the larynx, then the
   babbling begins,
then the echoes,
the howling during cold days you spend alone with wolves.
But to talk over long distances, requires the formation of song,
the way a bird hears itself sing."
My father was the same way,
singing to himself, I thought.
Even when I was hoisted above his shoulders,
on our way to deliver illegal substances,
white powders he said made people feel like the happiest ponies ever born.
The man with a bouquet of flowers for a head
married one of my father's ex-girlfriends.
I was the flower girl at their wedding.
During the toast
someone pulled a crank on the top of their head
to open a passage in the skull,
revealing an ocean inside,
a pod of dolphins leaping.

SHANE McCRAE

Explaining My Appearance in Certain Pictures

In pictures now I do not smile and didn't

Then, I would laugh if I was being tickled

And sometimes one, my mother's mother would tick-

le me, and the   other would take the picture

My mother's father, and so sometimes I'm

Not smiling but I'm laughing, my eyes closed

And my mouth open, almost like I'm scream-

ing, but I'm laughing,   when I was a child

In pictures with my kidnappers, with one

My mother's mother always her.   I'm sitting

Most often in her lap, her arms around

My blurred   waist, she has me on rita-

lin, and the trick   is wait until

The laughing stops.   As the mouth closes you can take the smile

Far Past the End

After the first few months or after how

-ever long, after   they my mother's parents

Stopped taking   pictures of me looking happy

As if against the day

They would need pictures of me looking happy

To get a lighter sentence,   I remember

Nothing of what in the first months after happened

But still I must have been

Dying, I had been   taken from my life

My life I don't   remember once remembering

Still I was   three and I   must have been happy

Sometimes, and even with them

My mother's parents, who had kidnapped me

Dying but sometimes hungry, sleepy

Sometimes, and even when   I missed my father, must have

Wanted to play, even when

I still remembered what he looked like, what his

Voice sounded like.   How happy must you keep the

Child you have kidnapped if you want

Him to forget?   or clap

How loud each time he turns his head to look

At something you can't see   in the doorway? How

Far past the end of the old life is the end

Of the living memory

The Fungus Called Dead Man's Fingers

It's true, the fungus does look like a dead man's fingers

Look   at a picture of the fungus if you don't believe

Me, or a dead   woman's, it's true, if how we think

The dead man died was he was murdered, and he reaches

From the heart of the earth imploring,   or it might as well be

The heart of the earth, six   feet below the surface, for

How clear the grave is when I try to picture it

How clear the heart where men lie   is, if he was killed

By love, once love, said   it was love, not

The love that packed the body in the heart of the earth, not

The last   love, that informed or instigated the concern

To see the body buried, to see the gray cheeks blushed

Before the grave winch married it to the earth, not

The love at the beginning of the chain of un

-doing being, love waving   at itself and us, of the chain of not

Revivifying, but   of gesturing toward life, a burying

Love, but a love that hides   in the crowd at the funeral, its face

Small, like the face of a boy, cross-armed, sitting in

A plastic chair in the hall outside the murmuring

Door   with the boy who punched him, small   but powerfully

Alone now,   how a boy will use his wound

To make his way in the world, like an impossible

Omnidirectional red carpet now unfurling

Backwards through time, from the theater to the limo, from

His future loves to his eye swollen shut

If we imagine it was love that killed the dead man

Said it was love,   whose fingers reach from the heart of the earth

Toward you, the dead man is a woman and you know her

The Dead Negro in the Modernist Long Poem

To decorate your poems with our deaths

Bodies of rivers being black flesh in water

And bones in flesh, loosed   from the threatening muscles

      Unknowable as laughter

In rooms in which the laughter stops   the moment

You enter,   where the faces are all faces

Of who will soon be dead, although they live

      Dead in a poem, and faceless

Hanging from the tree of knowledge   at the source

Poet, of your childhood shame, of the branchéd river

It is a hanging tree where it begins

      Of which you are the flower

PHILIP GROSS

Early Nocturne, Penarth Head

In the beginning God said, Let there be
surfaces. That was the deep invention.
Mere profundity came later.
      And he blessed them with light

like today – late January sun
tired by a whole day's outing
lies along the sixty miles of estuary,
      its blue mild as a sigh

reaching into itself to find an almost
yellow. Tenderness: to see that water,
which will proverbially "close over us"
      without a thought, has memory:

the still swish, slightly widening
like a lazy contrail, in a boat's wake,
which persists, the silvery-matt pallor
      of a well-healed scar,

when the boat and its blunt nudge
of ripples have gone. The feeling skin
of things. How that contour line of dark,
      some way offshore, recalls

each corrugation of the last high
tide-wrack or anticipates the next. World
without end: no limit to the times, love,
      we've said, Look, and look –

my notating each nuance of light. So
much seeing and saying, we could be
spreading out to depthlessness,
        pure surface and yes,

we're going nowhere. This is everywhere to go.

The Named Storm

            ... there, beside me, me and three or four
cold others on the hopeless platform, each of them with names
I'd never know,
        the named storm waiting, sullen, with us,
with late getting later, and the indicator board
out of excuses. Could this have been our doing: we had called her
by name?

      Now it's night; I'm home; the named storm too
is home; she's roaming round the garden – not a single flood
of presence but the here-and-there of her, one moment
in the alley round the back, bad-whispering;
                the next,
in the trees like a flock of herself, dispersed along the branches
and ready to fly, with her hundred-mile cries.

             No consolation
to be told that soon she'll have blown herself out,
nor-nor-east; that she'll be losing her identity, off somewhere
I too am forgetting, some cape, some ness, some Viking
vowel,
     to be a crackle in our radio reception, the lights
flickering, her absence still more *here* for being named.

KATHRYN MARIS

Because I too feel the violence of ▓▓▓▓▓ I do not insert myself into conflicts

On the train especially three thoughts occur to me:
the English countryside is a perfectly violent place,
Shall I put the kettle on is a strange little insult,
and maybe moderation is a version of excess
(though I don't think I've ever been excessive?)
Oh God oh God oh God oh... sunlight is salubrious.
I must stop taking things in:
there's a chronic blockage in my throat.
The sky completely changed while we were talking
so I used the opportunity to clarify, but was concise.
He said he thought he *was* being nice
when I had the awful realisation...
My father's favourite unquantifiable is currency,
my daughter's is microplastics in fish;
and I am filling my own desolation with tonic + gin.
When I looked at my reflection in the well,
I remembered boring everyone, which I did
less when I was ignorant and attractive.
I am not so stupid as you might think:
more than one side of this country wants me
dead – even you, in the well, at your most
and least animal, in this furtively violent place.
I recall I believed I was being poisoned
by that decent man who was so maternal
(I didn't voice my suspicion but swapped plates).
I have started to worry again about poison
and I talk about it a lot, about poison.
I was so moved to be told *You are not a monster*
because, of course, I am inclined to accept the role,
or any role that is offered me, in this or any urban or
rural scene, a rural scene/sweet especial rural scene

on which I vomit these fragments:
every capitalist nanoparticle
as bourgeois as the monolith from which it came.

Echopoem

I won't be caught personifying nature

When I ask *Do the fish seem happy?*

What I mean is *Have I killed them yet with metaphors?*

I sometimes confuse my dog with my sweater

But the dog is not "mine" nor must it accept

A pretentious mythological name

I could have given my child

Were I ballsy enough

So I name him "Frank" after Helen Frankenthaler

God said we'd have dominion over Dog

(Please allow my mistranslation to make a point)

Ecstatic lyricism is a construct of only human nature

There are more Schrödinger's Cats than anyone knows

And as long as we make hierarchical distinctions between lyric and
  other poetic forms

We might as well argue against biodiversity

Let there be no one alive but poets!

This is an earnest ecopoem really

I took a selfie in front of a tree

The image that appeared on the phone

Was of me in the stocks

Then me typing a caption

This is me hurling stones at myself in the stocks

A child feeds some koi in a too-small pond

Calling out their names: Virgil, Milton, Blake, Wordsworth, Hopkins,
    Hughes...

The child wrote a poem about a fly

It buzzed

But had no other transcendental function

MELISSANTHI, *translated by Kathryn Maris*

Narcissus

Who knows the true story of Narcissus
Dreaming of beauty,
Bowing down to meet his own face
In the pond, watching leaves
In an upside-down watery sky,
Shadow and light in deceptive opposition
All day and all night
Dreaming, afraid of his reflection
The empty gaze
               – trapped in its bubble
Suggestive of death
Of a body so beautiful in life
So full of rot, so disgusting, in death
Despair bent and drowned him in the end
Because, just as in dreams and fiction,
Where everything is itself and something else,
Death and life are basically the same
Like all things in the world, our soul
Is one thing and also its reverse
Like the tree – in and out of the pond

RACHAEL ALLEN

from *God Complex*

Listening, always.
Now it won't be.

A pint of bark is incorrect.

A bit between my teeth you gallop me around like an animal.
Dallied pet.

If you are pushed to a breaking point as you like being used
but you cannot say it, hand pressed over a red-hot grate.

Your abuser's mother telling you
about the things she did
that may explain his behaviour

. . .

My fault – I want men to find me so attractive
they want to end my life.

This is the most flattering and lasting gift bestowed upon
the women in my history
they were so loved it calcified white to hate.

   I have felt it
(both the want to kill and to be killed)
being so loved it turns to threat – don't tell me otherwise
 – is the truest

        this is what I have come to accept.

          Sometimes I feel the edges of my teeth bleed and taste
metal in my mouth, like a big iron dick.
I ignore it like
I've been ignored in an unreciprocated *I love you*
sitting in my mouth like an uncomfortable cloud, growing bigger
and sharper, the kind that covers
the sun while you swim
the turbulence kind
you can only wish it away

                              . . .

I used to look up and feel the earth
come apart in my stomach
with power or potential; not now,
you have closed me.

Petri dish exclamations, your mood
is a hard bound hand against me
and my hands bound hard behind me, against wood.

I live by your mood, an operational system.

How overcome is the day?
Between green veils and a tendril of thought.

The mapping of abuse, travelling through
a stem system that goes both
backwards and forwards in time.

I take solace elsewhere,
but the person I look to for love
is the horse's bit between my teeth
like ancient dentistry or torture

Is it
being thrown through a window as a grown woman
thrown through a grown window as a changed man
thrown through the grown woman, a good window

      or, growing the limbs of
dead relatives
we still conjure through our throats –
     murdered by a love
branch as a tongue –

This is the pattern of deaths we carry, marked in our bodies as bands.
Bands in our thinking as the bands of a tree show age
and our teeth show that grey trauma
unable to shake the mark that serrated or the mark that conjured
through it the holographic spectre of who died and when.

     To fall in love time and time again with the species of her murderer,
     inescapable, inexcusable, without explanation and I cannot
     remove myself from the pattern

       . . .

Ego ridden I am shot through with it
like a man gone to war shot through to his knees

take this unholy and asphyxiated environment
and star it with a galaxy more generous than this

the photons of an ancient time that have built to
nothing but modern cruelty, which now capsize through

a metabolism we crank and dissect

and fuss, with new foods grown in tanks and labs
labs where they pin mice by their legs to slabs

and number them into the billions
slaughter grows exponentially like maths, like slaughter

like the expanding furious galaxy, and god's hand
in it like a Petri dish

of creatures, inconsequential and so of consequence.

    My old friend's dead father held my name in the

    back of a journal he kept. Who knows what we inhabit
in this, pinned to the darkness, numbered animals

    . . .

I lived with a grief so deep I'd have scooped that plasticity up
chewed through just to feel something.

Days spent wandering along the party river.

Hen-do masks floating mask-side-up in the dark brown –
feathers sprouting from the tip.

Rat-sweetened water.

I was the colour of a pale house on fire – pink at the edges, the colour of a
blackened lung frozen then defrosted – pink in the middle.

And yes I'd walk around that city like a trailing plague
and I loved it.

I would love and fuck every wall in my mania; even the deeply ancient ones,
even the Roman ones!

In this pain I was a charred donkey in the office chair – stupid and unusual.

I'd have whole conversations with myself pretending half of me was you.
I was so alone so deeply all there was was river

and dome of inexplicable smoke in the sky

GOLIARDA SAPIENZA, *translated by Brian Robert Moore*

from *Ancestral*

Another Fairy Tale

The withered bodies of the deceased
are all around us. In the evenings
they walk by our side on the road
they bend over us while we read
watch us from afar if we talk with
a girlfriend, sitting by the front door.
Are you afraid of their
gaze from the past?
I too am afraid but I also fear
breathing while I sleep
and scattering into the air
the paper tissue of their faces
fixated on our repose
between the dawn and the day of this
bodily hour.

It's true there's not
much we can do.
You iron the bedsheets
on the mattress. With your hand you
flatten every crease. I pour water
from a glass
onto the balcony's burnt geraniums. It's true
there are not
many roads to go down
nor dead to pick from.
The only thing's to toss
the coin and watch
heads or tails.

You kill me but my face
will remain ingrained as glass
in your gaze.
Cutting. During the night
your pinned-down eyelids
will tear.

Do not go stay
the air freezes all
around my hands
Cracks run through the mirrors
The blue in your eyes
has empty spaces of
steel. Behind you renewed
waiting flings open the halls.
And I don't have the strength
to go down them again
I don't have the strength
to drag myself on all fours
along the walls.

YVONNE REDDICK

Esther in the Asylum Garden

*I walked with Valerie a while, down the familiar labyrinth of shovelled
asylum paths.*
  – Sylvia Plath, *The Bell Jar*

To be born twice, clamber to the fig-tree's summit. Swaying
in the branch-sea, you'll realise how snappable the neck's stem is,
but you won't slip, Esther. The Carmelite sister and the rabbi
– you know the yarn? Imagine this tree was theirs. She'd
pry orbs of ripeness from the twigs; he'd raise them to his lips.

Moss-carders, carpenters, miner bees: the females labour to quicken
hipless roses, whir to their nunnish cells at sundown. They outwit
aerial nets and kill-jars. But the fig's unseen flower teems with wasps.
A skep of stings. Queens enter the unripe ovary, tear
their wedding-veil wings; the tree pairs them with its prisoned males.

Tell me, whose mind isn't a fizzing hive of venom? I'm sick
of freezing baths, Doc Quinn droning on about Freud, Dad, death.
The wallpaper in these rooms is a migraine, but I'm glad you're here –
remember wading through *Finnegans Wake*, then bourbon with Yalies?
Here, they'll treat me with shocks of metrazol or insulin.

Salvia once salved wounds; feverfew was a febrifuge. Listen: the loon's
tremolo, *cheer-up cheerily* of robins. The fig-tree endures
lightning that blitzes through its crown. Come fall, the fruit will wink,
wine-purple with knowledge. Pick one that splits, and you'll bite hearts.
A globed one for Lyon, Ravenna, El Arabí: countries close as health.

That bracelet of bruised fingermarks on your wrist has healed;
you've survived entrées laced with poison, those forty
barbiturates you swallowed. Your line will live beyond the final page.
We'll climb the espalier, drive all night to Elm Street, begin
the rite to plant our second spring – come now with me.

IAN DUHIG

Tine

I am the deer of sixteen tines,
more than your Monarch of the Glen,
I set horns on the heads and words in the brains
of women and men.

Tine means fire in tine an mhadra rua:
foxfire, will o' the wisp or jack o' lantern;
my lights breathe out on your page-white moor
where poems burn.

I am time fled from Hallaig wood,
your seconds are my second-hand clothes;
you walk through curtains of hide for the word
no human knows.

I am the deer of many points
all too dark for your brightest mind:
the point of poetry, of arguments, of weapons
and of being kind.

My dark blood fills your books,
the white of my eye behind each page
looks beyond where your poet or sorcerer looks
to curse your age.

Pheasant's Eye

A poem is a pheasant, Wallace Stevens wrote:
it makes footprints like time's arrows pointing
backwards, from here to those I once followed
over new snow which suddenly stopped dead.

Fox? No foxprints. Thought fox then? I stared
at the blank page of this field so long, it grew
as foxed as I with patches where bulbs stirred,
preparing to happen or not, unmade by poetry.

What I don't know about pheasants would fill
a library of Borgesian size. Take down a book.
Open it anywhere, see the ghost of the nothing
not there and nothing that is, the white sheet

a picnic cloth over bulbs of narcissi poetici,
the poet's narcissus, known as pheasant's eye.

An Arbitrary Light Bulb

Under Sewerby Hall's Lantern of Demosthenes
I found a pebble the exact shape of a light bulb.
Then, suddenly, as if in one of my old *Beanos*,
another lit above my head in a thought bubble

trailing diminuendo echoes, like Little Plum's
smoke signals, to my dull bulb of skull below
until they disappeared into that unplumbable
nothing where so many of my poem ideas go.

I sucked this stone like a pear drop in the hope
it might hatch a poem, or seed one, but so far
nothing worth the light, the idea's bulb blown
to an abandoned oratory that never had a prayer.

I spat it out, but the hole it left was a gift to me
beyond all rhetoric to figure, or poetry to sing,
reminding me that shape was called an 'arbitrary':
an arbitrary light bulb, was the name of the thing.

TIM LIARDET

When I Hear Mr Blum, the Funeral Director,

has been located ten blocks from home in his longjohns,
has overdosed on alprazolam and his toe is stubbed and purple.
When I hear of his daughters Joslyn, Orit and Nimah
who always wear those butterfly nets over their three faces.
When I hear what is stored in the freezer truck outside
and how in the muck that clings to the tailgate a finger
has written in lopsided capitals: THE DEAD ARE INSIDE.
When I hear a birdcage elevator's not a lift so much
as a stash of Amazon boxes that are their own installation.
When I hear Ms Smolar, the gaunt mortician, confessing
she no longer feels she is able to dress the deceased
in their hoedown dresses or to brush or comb their hair.
When I hear how Ms Smolar and Mr Blum already are all out
of eye-caps and suture-strings, greasepaints and powder,
all out of body-bags, all out of space. All out of aorta.
When I hear there's a job lot of mortuary lipstick pledged
at the depot but when it arrives it's all pickle green.
When I imagine Adorno's typewriter in arrest,
all tangled up in its locked, arthritic hand of keys.
When I hear there's a heap of spectacles growing,
all snarled up in its wires, its temple tips and hinges.
When I hear Mister Yudin, the cousin of Mr Blum
and Ms Smolar's brother, the one who keeps the books,
has grown so face-blind he is plagued by every face,
in each of them I find my father's face in death:
I think of the crease of his brow, converging on kindness,
on the mannerly spot that seemed to be his home.
I see his sinking away, like something released,
the last tiniest flare of his flesh consigned
to the dark of the bag as the zip closed over his face.

KAREN McCARTHY WOOLF

from *un/safe*

O England, boasted land of liberty,
With strangers still thou mayst thy title own
But thy poor slaves the alteration see
With many a loss to them the truth is known
    – John Clare, 'The Village Minstrel'

At a time when gentrification was intensifying in London, and elsewhere around the world—

At a time when state violence against black, brown and working-class bodies continues to intensify, I started to think tattoos were a new territorial act—

I started to think a tattoo was a way to reclaim agency over the body as our access to and freedoms within public space diminished—

. . .

For a long time I found it difficult to process the aesthetic ambivalence of tattoos. As in some tattoos look shit. This made me think more about tattoos. And I became convinced they were a response to a larger, contemporary land grab.

. . .

          I'm surprised that I'm surprised
to learn tattoos are *haram*
      & discouraged in Leviticus 19:28
is it innate

                   the urge
                   to fill that which
                   appears
                   to be
                   empty ?
      that which was never empty

Photo: Karen McCarthy Woolf

barbed

               mangling weapon
       invented & deployed by settlers
       to shape & control

       space
       as appropriated by settler states
       (—so many of them, all vigorously resisting
       transparency
       instead urging the opaque)

wire

       with which America's plains were wrangled & wrested
       with which
       & from whom

             & Whereas

                . . .

A tattoo is also
a musical term,
is defined as
"any drumming
or tapping".
From the
Dutch: "tap-
toe", meaning
to close the tap
on the cask.
A tattoo is a
military term.
A bugle
sounds and
soldiers
gather—

Photo: Karen McCarthy Woolf

. . .

& it occurs that we are entering a new & revived idiomatic era

Of Incarceration

Of lockdown
(a phrase I first encountered in a library, a prison library)

Of curfew
(a mangling of medieval French, of an order, to cover the
fire, *couvre* as in cover, few as in *feu*, after a certain hour, to put
the fire out, so no fire might gleam or crackle in the dark)

Of *your country needs you* to—

& that it was a prison library, a prison
     where tattoos are banned
     &   prevalent—a punctuation
     a puncture that denotes
          time: two dots, three dots, four dots, five &

where inmates are entangled   on the wires
        of a spider's web

. . .

The tattoo is also a musical term. The tattoo is a tapping.

. . .

& skin is music &
         music is skin is music is
    skin is music is skin
is music is skin is

        a tap tap tapping

&

SYLVIA LEGRIS

Pomegranate, Carthaginian Apple

A wild pomegranate tree.
A tree that promises to explode.

Fruit as fragmenting bomb.
Fruit of the many-seeded dead.

Seeds of semiprecious provenance.
Seeds that detonate garnet.

Flowers that yield astringent dye.
Flowers that yield harsh nectar.

Nectar that keeps loose teeth fastened.
Nectar that stops the blood-spitter spitting.

A quick-witted pomologist gobs a spitball.
A fruitful pomologist lobs an apple-grenade.

Divine blood- and fire-filled.
Wind flowers and thunder claps.

Mercury offers up rain and tricks.
Mercury offers up subterfuge and flash.

Hare

1

The land hare eats the hare's-foot fern for lunch.
A hare both herbaceous and herbivorous.
The rabbit's foot is a plant in prayer.
Low-lying, nocturnal.
A decumbent hare.

2

Apicius ranked entrées of hare second only to peacock.
An earth hare in earthenware.
A jugged hare.
A stewed in blood hare.
A hare pfeffered and braised.
A cat rousted from a roof and roasted as a hare.

3

The art of the hare is the art of not-showy blooms.
A drove of shrubby hares in well-drained soil.
A scroll of simple recipes.
First catch your hare.
Then RSVP the bees.

Sheathfish [sic]

A close cousin of Aristotle's catfish,
stoic sheathfish makes the voice sing.

A fish who sings adversity and enigma.
A fish who sings cooling pond and catastrophe.

"Freshwater or sarcophagus?" sings sheathfish.
"Eyeshine or particle emission?" sheathfish sings.

"Chuck the zone of alienation!
Who's the bottom-feeding top predator now?"

Sling mud at the mud cat, chuckle at the chucklehead,
charmed sheathfish makes the charged waters sing.

Earthworm

Dew-worm, rainworm, angleworm.
The annelidical worm who questions the soil.
The reciprocal worm who aerates the earth.
The skin-breathing worm (the gas-exchanger).
The mathematical worm who measures the depth.
The worm who cures both earache and toothache.
The worm who glues sinews torn apart.
Hence a small song for the multitasking worm.

Map of Medical Materials (Province of Saskatchewan with Dioscorides)

The words on the map, as they appear:

Burnt Brass Sea Lavender, Wild Marsh Beet
Zinc Oxide Teazle Wild Feverwort
Cadmium Earth Bears Breeches Sea Artemisia Earthgall
Burnt Red Earth 5.170. GE (Earth) Iron Slag Silver Slag Apple of Earth Rhapontic
Laminated Rock Black Coral Rust Silver Salts and Gold Salts Burnt Lead
Fossilised Oyster Shells
Adamantine
Spar
Gather the herb to heal whitlows Turpentine Tree like wild horminum Herb
when dung with vinegar of Grace
the herb in the spring at sunrise 3-2. RA
Cockroach Blatta orientalis Bald-money Meu, Spignel, Bear Root
Punica granatum Grime from the gymnasium walls
Grime from the baths translates as the lungs of the sea Juniperos vulgaris
grows among the leaves are POISONOUS Acorus odoratus Sorbus domestica
rocks Grime from the wrestling school
Poet's Narcissus Squill
Black Nightshade
4-21. SPARGANION
Sweet Maudlin Stinking Motherwort
Perfoliate Honeysuckle Devil's Apple
Woundwort Periwinkle Aconite
Liverwort Running Myrtle
Jacob's Ladder
Hare's Foot Mercury's Violet
the blood of Hercules Pomegranate
windiness around the ears Carthaginian Apple
like little daggers Sheath Fish Sepia officinalis Cuttlefish
Ass's Liver Cimex lectularius — Bed Bugs Lungs of Swine Sea Centipedes
the stomach 2.25. ORCHIS HIPPOPOTAMOU Horse Tongue Liquid from Salt Fish
river snail is poisonous
Love in a Mist earth snail
Devil in a Bush Rush Nut
Acorns Sweet Flag Myrtle Sedge
Quercus Feather Grass
Purging Croton
Saffron Crocus Gall Oak Dyer's Oak
Water Snowflake
Sweet Rush Oleaster
Spikenard
1-1. IRIS Nut Gall Oak
piper apum HazelwortHorse Elder Nut Common
Sword Lily Papaver rhoeas [Linnaeus] Goat's
Flowers of Brass Field Poppy Marsh Valerian Rue
Blue Flower de Luce Corn Rose Corn Poppy Hare

Topography of Repeating Plants and Patterns
(Province of Saskatchewan with William Morris)

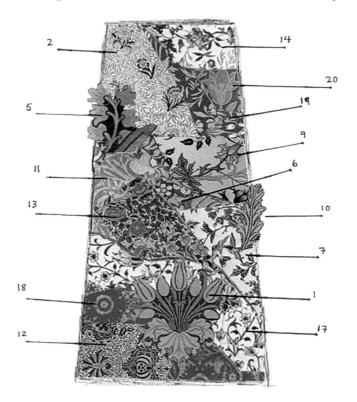

Yard Goods: Remnants

Legend

1. Tulips among a grass of worsted warp.
2. Leaves peppered with carnations and peonies.

3. Honeysuckle and myrtle (one entwines linen, one adorns a wall).
4. Sunflower and acanthus leaves in a garden of combed cotton and silk.

5. Block-printed bluebells on cotton and linen.
6. A simple appliqué design of pomegranates and foliage.

7. Elegantly worked trees with hopelessly stylized birds.
8. Branches of hummingbird and crested bird on printed cotton.

9. Honeysuckle and briar on cream-colored ground.
10. A design of curving leaves.

11. Vine and pomegranates on 3-ply carpeting.
12. Pomegranates and foliage in pink and green silk.

13. Rosebush and apple tree cushion covers.
14. Morning glory and bindweed (*convolvulus*) cushion covers.

15. Artichokes and thistles in gold thread and silk.
16. A 4-part mohair colorway of violet and columbine.

17. Daffodil-, willow bough-, and rambling rose-printed cotton.
18. Acorn embossed on silk velvet.

19. Medieval designs with sunflowers and daisies.
20. Dyes as old as Pliny: chestnut, plum, saffron, madder.

Essay

LISTENING FOR STARS

Mina Gorji

Late at night. Everyone has gone to bed. You are sitting listening to the quiet. Now and then your ear picks up the hum of the fridge in the kitchen. The washing machine begins its final frantic acceleration, like a rocket preparing to launch. It is just after midsummer. Outside, the stars are silent. Venus has returned to the northern hemisphere. Gradually, fainter stars begin to emerge as your eyes get used to the dark. And your ears tune in to quiet. Listening out into that vast quiet distance. The stars are silent from where we stand. A pale moon appears. It is a new moon, a crescent moon, a quiet moon as it was once called.

Samuel Taylor Coleridge had an ear tuned to quiet. Sitting up alone late at night in November 1803, he recorded his listening in a notebook: the ticking of his watch, "& the far lower note of the noise of the Fire— perpetual, yet seeming uncertain". He hears in the faint crackle of the fire "the low voice of quiet change", the voice "of Destruction doing its work by little & little". Listening to quiet.

In his great poem 'Frost at Midnight', written in February 1798, under a new moon, Coleridge is listening. And inviting us to listen with him. To the silence of frost on a windless night. Broken by the call of an owlet. His ear notices that it's an owlet, rather than an owl. A young owl. Inside the cottage, it is calm. His baby son Hartley slumbers in his arms. The poem that emerges is a listening meditation. Listen.

> The Frost performs its secret ministry,
> Unhelped by any wind. The owlet's cry
> Came loud—and hark, again! loud as before.
> The inmates of my cottage, all at rest,
> Have left me to that solitude, which suits
> Abstruser musings: save that at my side
> My cradled infant slumbers peacefully.
> 'Tis calm indeed! so calm, that it disturbs
> And vexes meditation with its strange
> And extreme silentness. Sea, hill, and wood,
> This populous village! Sea, and hill, and wood,
> With all the numberless goings on of life,
> Inaudible as dreams! the thin blue flame
> Lies on my low burnt fire, and quivers not;
> Only that film, which fluttered on the grate,
> Still flutters there, the sole unquiet thing.
> Methinks, its motion in this hush of nature
> Gives it dim sympathies with me who live,
> Making it a companionable form,
> Whose puny flaps and freaks the idling Spirit
> By its own moods interprets, every where
> Echo or mirror seeking of itself,
> And makes a toy of Thought.

That repeated word "loud", describing the "owlet's cry", primes our ears, or rather, our *mind's ear*, or what Robert Frost called the *imagining ear*, to listen for a certain pitch of sound, heightening the shift into quiet that follows. Through the calm, the "strange and extreme silentness", a thin blue flame comes into focus. Perfectly still. Not a quiver. Like the string of a lute, silent in stillness. Only the film of soot is moving now, fluttering on the grate, not still as in *quiet*, but, with a slight adjustment, *still fluttering*, moving, continuing to move, against the grate of the fire. It is "the sole unquiet thing".

   Coleridge invites us to listen and to think, and think again, about the music of quiet, and the words we use to describe it. Peaceful. Calm. Still. Hush. Dim. Secret. That word "secret" in the very first line of the poem would have suggested quiet to Coleridge's first readers, since "secret" carried the sense, no longer current, of reticence, of quiet and closeness (keeping something close, keeping it secret). A secret is unsounded. Silent. The frost "performs a secret ministry". We do not *hear* the icy patterns forming on the windowpane. Nor do we hear the poem's first rhyme, between "ministry" and "cry", it is an eye rhyme, silent.

Then, through that icy silence, an owlet's cry. We feel as though we're standing with Coleridge, listening with him as we shift from past tense "came loud" to the present "hark, again!", moving from the distance of the past to the immediacy of HARK, give ear, listen! But to what? To the owlet. And then, the quiet. To the calm breathing of a baby. To the "strange and extreme silentness", *inaudible as dreams*, to the flutter of soot, to the silence of icicles, and the quiet of the moon. The poem's last lines imagine sounds beyond the frosted windowpane:

> whether the eave-drops fall
> Heard only in the trances of the blast,
> Or if the secret ministry of frost
> Shall hang them up in silent icicles,
> Quietly shining to the quiet Moon.

That word "heard" alerts us. To the sound of water dripping from the eaves, only audible in the "trances of the blast", in the quiet pauses between gusts of wind. "[T]rances" suggests a state of suspension; Coleridge is using a term that describes a state of human consciousness, a liminal state, "between sleeping and waking; [...] a stunned or dazed state" (OED), to describe the rhythm of the wind, the quiet between blasts, and doing so subtly conveys the mesmerising experience of listening. This is suggested in the rhythmic patterning of the line as well as semantically: there is a delicate shift of emphasis in the phrase "**tran**ces of the", with its three unstressed beats in a row after **tran** (*-ces of the*) suggesting a quieting before the stressed word "**blast**" sounds at the end of the line. This moment of absorbed, focused listening prepares us for the distant echo in the next line. We are back to that "secret ministry of frost" we heard at the start of the poem. But now the frost is hanging up the water drops "in silent icicles". Silent, because they no longer splash like water drops between "the trances of the blast". They are frozen. "Silent icicles".

That word "silent" invites our listening. Our ears become subtly attuned to the sounds of the word *silence* itself, which shifts, thaws gently into quiet. The line "quietly shining to the quiet moon", picks up, echoes back, the *i* sound repeated in *silent icicles*, recalling the sound of that word *silence* even as it suggests something different. Quiet, not silent. It's not, as it might have been, *silently* shining to the *silent* moon, but *quietly* shining to the *quiet* moon; and this shift suggests a slight adjustment, a thawing of *silence* into quiet sound. Because although *quiet* can sometimes mean silent, it usually suggests a low or subdued sound. *Quietly shining to the quiet moon.* As *quietly* dims into the shorter *quiet*, it draws our ear to listen in again, to the possibility of the moon's quiet sound. How can we hear the moon across vast distances of sky? And as the distance opens up, the poem itself recedes. That last line is shorter, missing a stress. So that instead of the five-stress line our ears have become used to, here there are only four, **quiet**ly **shin**ing to the **quiet moon**. And we are left both with a sense of lack and anticipation, as we listen out for the missing stress. Listening in to the silence.

And it's this impossible listening, for a sound that we can never hear, which stirs imagination. A great poet, Coleridge explained, in a letter to his friend William Sotheby, should be able to listen with "the ear of a wild Arab listening in the silent Desart". Listening. But for what? It is the state of listening itself, this hearkening that Coleridge is describing. Listening at night in his cottage in Nether Stowey, under a quiet moon, he invites us to listen too.

· · ·

the first whisper of stars is a faint thing

Down the road, metal ears are listening for stars. One of the first radio telescopes – the 4C Array – was built here, on the outskirts of Cambridge, in the 1950s. Captured German radio antennae repurposed to hear the faintest signals from space, radio waves sent out light-years ago, picked up like a whisper. In her poem 'A Star Here and a Star There', Alice Oswald tunes her ears to the frequency of stars:

the first whisper of stars is a faint thing
a candle sound, too far away to read by

the first whisper of stars is a candle sound
those faraway stars that rise and give themselves airs
      a star here and a star there
the first whisper of stars is that faint thing
that candle sound too faint to read by

when you walk outside leaving the door ajar
and smell the various Danks of Dusk
      and a star here
      and a star there

Star sound carried across vast distances, amplified by the poet's imagining ear, to the intimacy of a whisper, "a faint thing", a candle's gentle sputter, "too faint to read by". Moving between eye and ear, light and sound, the poem explores what it means to perceive stars, shifting scale and register, oscillating between far away and intimate. 'A Star Here and a Star There' is the first of the concluding sequence of poems in Oswald's third collection *Woods etc.* (2005) that explore the further reaches of our skies, from moon to the deep silence of space, including 'Moon Hymn', 'Various Portents', 'Excursion to the Planet Mercury', and 'Sonnet', the final poem in the collection, which describes "Spacecraft Voyager 1 boldly gone / into Deep Silence".

In 'A Star Here and a Star There', the stars move in and out of our ken, in and out of focus. Oswald creates a sense of distance in a number of ways, shifting font size, for instance. In the first half of the poem she uses a smaller typeface for the repeated words from the title, a phrase that flickers and repeats in variations, transforming as it goes: "a star here / and a star there [...] and a star / here and there / and / here and there the / start of a". At first we hear it like the trace of a refrain, then like a message sounding intermittently, fading in and out. The smaller type creates a sense of distance, of visual perspective, giving the impression that these stars are smaller somehow, further away.

Oswald creates dynamic shifts of scale in other ways too, moving between linguistic registers, from the close domestic familiarity of the

candle and its faint whisper, to the exotic names of faraway stars, those
stars that rise "and give themselves airs":

> – Alkaid Mizar Alioth –
> trying to make you hear who they once were
> and a star
> here and there
> and
> here and there the
> start of a
> Phad Merak Muscida – it's like blowing a ring of cinders
> all that sky that lies hidden in the taken for granted air

"Alkaid Mizar Alioth" are the names of stars that make up what's
commonly known as the Big Dipper in Ursa Major. The tail of the
Great Bear, Alkaid is its most easterly star, one of the brightest in
the night sky. Alkaid is also one of the fifteen Behenian stars used in
medieval magic rituals; its name appearing in the poem introduces
an incantatory, mysterious quality. "Phad Merak Muscida", the names
of more stars in Ursa Major, appear a few lines later, interrupting the
simple linguistic register ("Here and there the / start of a"), so that the
poem's language moves from the familiar to the faraway, like a radio
shifting between stations, from the everyday words "here and there",
to another more mysterious and higher linguistic frequency, before
shifting back to the familiar and the bodily, "it's like blowing a ring of
cinders". From the further reaches of Ursa Major, back to the closeness
of the breath, and the warmth of cinders. The repeated *in* sounded in
"blowing", "ring" and "cinders" suggests the flare-up of light in sound,
but also the flickering of a star far away, a moment of brightness, and
then hesitation: will the ring of cinders light up, fade, flicker?

The repetition of words in the poem also suggests the intermittent
light of stars seen across vast distances and time, "here and there / and
/ here and there the". There is a flicker of rhythm, not quite gathering,
patterns almost repeated, hinted, half-heard, the whispering flicker of a
star. That unexpected word "hear" in "trying to make you hear who they
once were" (how can a star make you hear?) is echoed in the repeated
"here" in "here and there / and / here and there", drawing our ear

across the lines, and to the trace of *star* in "start". The fragility of starlight viewed from our distant planet is played out and suggested across the sounds the poem makes, patterns appearing, fading, reappearing slightly altered, so that the poem's shifts and flickerings serve as a vast receiving ear, a radio telescope picking up a signal far away, in and out of range.

Several of the poems in *Woods etc.* dramatise moments of listening: to stars, to the silence of clouds, to the rain crackling the air, to the smack of a skimming stone as it contacts the water, to the sound of trees in the river ("put your ear to the river you hear trees"), and the sound of the river widening in trees ("put your ear to the trees"). To the sound of an owl:

> last night at the joint of dawn,
> an owl's call opened the darkness
>
> miles away, more than a world beyond this room
>
> and immediately, I was in the woods again,
> poised, seeing my eyes seen,
> hearing my listening heard

'Owl' is one of Oswald's finest explorations of listening. Here, "at the joint of dawn", she listens – not for an owl but for its *call*. The sound of that word *call* echoes the long *a* in *dawn*, giving the reader the sense of a double call, the doubled hooting of an owl. The poem plays with the doubling in various ways; in its sounds, but also in the doubling of perspective, so that the perceiving narrator becomes aware of being perceived, "seeing my eyes seen, / hearing my listening heard". This pattern of doubling also plays in and through the poem's sound patterns: that repeated *d* in *dawn* and *darkness* suggests another echoing call. The owl's call is not *sounded* in the darkness, it *opened* the darkness, and doing so it transforms the darkness into something material, something which can be opened, rather than simply an absence of light. Opens into what? The edge of the line. As our eyes move into the white space after "darkness", here is the possibility of dawn, flickering through the space between the poem's lines, the empty space where words might have been, a sense of distance opening between the lines as it describes a distance, "miles away, more than a world beyond this room".

Listening into space, into a pause, Oswald's line also listens back in time, remembering Wordsworth as "he hung / Listening", for an owl's answering cry at the end of a line. Listening to the silence. Suspended. Listening out for owls:

And, when there came a pause
Of silence such as baffled his best skill:
Then, sometimes, in that silence, while he hung
Listening, a gentle shock of mild surprise
Has carried far into his heart the voice
Of mountain-torrents; or the visible scene
Would enter unawares into his mind
With all its solemn imagery, its rocks,
Its woods, and that uncertain heaven received
Into the bosom of the steady lake.

Wordsworth, remembering his own listening. In these lines from 'There Was a Boy', which Wordsworth returned to and recast in *The Prelude*, the boy of Winander is listening. Suspended in the silence, he hears a voice. Not hears, but *receives*. It is the *voice* not of owls, but of *mountain-torrents*. And he receives this sound, this voice, not in his ears, but in his *heart*. Not *in* his heart, but *far into his heart*. Those short words *far* and *into* open up great distances: a voice travelling over the hills, across the valleys. Then the surprise intimacy of *heart*. At once *far off and near*. The listening heart. The heart transformed, expanded, opened up by listening. By the *voice of mountain waters*. A voice which disembodies. Which opens up great distances, transforms the heart's dimensions.

Reflecting on listening in her essay 'The Universe in time of rain makes the world alive with noise' (2000), Oswald describes it as

a way of forcing a poem open to what lies bodily beyond it. Because the eye is an instrument tuned to surfaces, but the ear tells you about volume, depth, content – like tapping a large iron shape to find if it's full or not. The ear hears into, not just what surrounds it. And the whole challenge of poetry is to keep language open, so that what we don't know yet can pass through it.

In 'Owl', the densely echoic language of the poem opens up the visceral experience of owl sound:

> then out, until it touched the town's lights,
> an owl's elsewhere swelled and questioned
>
> twice, like you might lean and strike
> two matches in the wind

Here the *ow* sound in *out* resounds, in *owl's*, and then, at least visually, the *w* and *l* in *owl's* recurs in *swelled*. The poem is dense in echoes; as well as the sound of the *owl* in these lines, the *e* in *elsewhere* returns in *swelled* and *questioned*. All of these repetitions are drawn out and amplified by that emphatic *twice*, appearing after a pause, at the start of a line, and emphasised by its placement above *two* in the next line, a semantic and acoustic echo at once. *Twice* is a key word in the poem, emphasised acoustically as it is underlined by repeated sounds, the *i* sound in *night*, *miles*, and in *strike* and echoing back the sound of *lights* from two lines earlier. The words *strike* and *lights* rhyme in sound and sense, since the *strike* of a match produces flame, and with it, *light*. And as our ear listens for echoes in the last line it picks up the *m* from *might* in *matches*, the *t* in *two* resounds the *t* in *twice* and the final repeated *in* in *in* and *wind*. But the poem's concluding line leaves us listening for a final sound, since it is just slightly – a syllable – shorter than we have come to expect; this lack, along with the absence of closing punctuation, leaves us listening for more, into the wind, into white space.

In a lecture about Ted Hughes given at Oxford University in November 2020, and available online, Oswald describes the white space at the end of a line as a listening space: "A good poem gives up its knowingness at the end of each line, inhales, listens and then starts again." The end of a line is figured as a moment of breathing, and of listening; the poem itself is listening, listening out, into the silence, into the whiteness of space; listening out for what will happen next.

> I love
> to stand among the last trees listening down
> to the releasing branches where I've been –

the rain, thinking I've gone, crackles the air
and calls by name the leaves that aren't yet there

These lines, this listening, is from Oswald's sonnet 'Wood not yet out'. The line break after "listening down" invites the reader to listen down to the next line, "to the releasing branches". That word "down" in "listening down" gives direction to an act which is not usually directed downwards: we don't usually "listen down the lane" as we might "look down the lane", more usually we listen *to* or *for* something, sometimes listen up, or, perhaps, we might just listen.

. . .

Jen Hadfield explores the spaces of listening a poem can offer in the concluding poem of *The Stone Age* (2021). In '(Sound travels so far)', the space opened up in parentheses becomes a listening space. This is a listening which takes place in parenthesis, and describes the way sound travels on a quiet, misty evening: "(Sound travels so far on the quiet evenings especially in mist". Are words held in parentheses quieter, sounded in a different key or tone, less emphatic? *Lunulae*: the word describes those crescent moon shapes bracketing words (...) in, out into a different voice, a different emphasis, a different time, a different volume? Not the main clause but an aside, quieter, perhaps. Several of the poems in *The Stone Age* use the parenthesis as a space for reflection, and Hadfield brackets out the titles too '(Lighthouse)', '(Erratic)', '(See how the leopard)', '(You said what you said)', '(Lunar transmission)', '(Fear opens)', '(Your tongue)', and '(Sound travels so far)', which only appear in the index and not above the poems themselves. The poems appear visually different from the others in the collection, printed in greyscale lettering of different shades and in varying sizes. Threading through the volume, they offer a change of pace and perception and shift how we read the poems in between.

In this short poem '(Sound travels so far)', Hadfield plays with greyscale font of various sizes to suggest a state of heightened listening. The typographic variances also register shifts of volume, amplification and diminuendo. Like Oswald, she plays with graphic codes for volume. If the shrinking font in 'A Star Here and a Star There' suggests distance and quiet, in her later long poem, 'Tithonus', from *Falling Awake* (2016),

Oswald uses fading coloured font to convey a dimming of sound, a visual language for quietening. In the poem's final lines, the ink gradually fades, so that the concluding word, "appearing", is almost invisible, printed in the very lightest shade of grey, as dawn, and light, appear. This fading out produces in visual language an aural effect, the suggestion of diminuendo, in the way that bold or capital letters, larger font size or italics can suggest a louder volume.

Hadfield takes this in a different direction. As we move through the evening poem, down the page, the size of the font increases and fades in colour to paler grey, as it describes sounds heard through the quiet, and through the mist: the strangely human cough of sheep and then, after the white space, we are drawn in to listen again; to the sound of a graveyard gate with its quiet hinge creaking. The increasing font size amplifies the intensity of the quiet sounds described, as if to bring the reader closer as we listen in; it is a kind of dramatic amplification, suggesting the way in which listening in quiet can intensify the sounds heard, heightening our experience of listening.

The size of the font increases again, and now swans (white) appear, and then a gap in the poem, a pause, white space, creating a sense of quiet suspense as we listen again in anticipation, before the poem shifts into another time. Hadfield plays with white space, indenting lines and adding space between lines instead of conventional punctuation to suggest pauses as well as shifts in sound:

and swans

on a still day
you hear the beat of their wings
something like the creaking of oars

a longboat rowed from the sky's shore
the hoarse cry of the oarsmen)

The poem's final image is not of the sound itself but an image of the sound, drifting through simile from bird to boat and out to sky's shore, the sound of *oars* sounding in *shore* and again in *hoarse* and *oarsmen*. That "hoarse cry of the oarsmen", reaches back into a distant Viking past. Hadfield lives on the isle of Shetland, which was colonised by Vikings in the ninth century. The poem describes how sound "travels so far", reaching back, through the "graveyard gate", back through the past, far back in time, across the evening and through the language.

Listening to the sounds of evening, Hadfield gestures at a longer Romantic tradition of evening-listening poems. Perhaps the best known of these is Gray's 'Elegy Written in a Country Churchyard', which opens with the toll of the "curfew bell", and travels through the sounds of evening into night, picking out the "lowing herd" and ploughman's "plod", the "droning flight" of the beetle, the "drowsy tinklings" of the distant fold, and the "moping owl" complaining to the moon. Hadfield's poem calls up a different soundscape, and uses graphic techniques to dramatise the sounds, and the experience of listening. She varies font size and colour and uses the white space to create shifts in perception, moments which invite and expand our listening. Framing the sounds of evening in parentheses, she develops a new kind of syntax and language for listening.

Playing with the visual presentation of the poem – with the expressive possibilities of white space, scale and shade – Hadfield and Oswald explore how poetry can translate the experience of listening into new forms. Coleridge too is interested in how poetry can enable and invite new ways of listening. His poem tunes in to the imaginative frequencies of quiet, but also to the ambiguities and histories of words. And he explores the ways in which stress patterns and rhythmic shifts communicate and suggest – not only to our ears and our mind's ears, but also somatically, drawing our bodies, our breathing, into new ways of thinking in and experiencing sound. These poems all begin with an act of listening – to the quiet of frost at midnight, to the cry of an owl, or the sounds of evening (heard through mist); but it is a listening that extends beyond the physiologically auditory – to where the imagining ear takes over – to hear the quiet of the moon, the voice of change, the distance of the past, the whisper of the stars.

EDWARD DOEGAR

from *I never thought it would come to this*

xvii.

Reflection wrongly
Applied justifies the
Meaning of an end

Time is running out
As the icon indicates
Even the sky can be

A futile understanding
That backs its own
Slo-mo disregard as

Rendered by panto-
Mime blue and bits
Of paper showing

Through the thin
Line of a surface
That society obscured

xviii.

To declare not belonging

Is a feeling of what isn't

Uncompromising myness

What remains is an intention

Even in writing these words

xix.

On the grounds that
It needs no further explanation
I can't explain
Anyway
The sense of too much

Of man's first disobedience
And all that
Inherited bullshit
That pertains
Still the pretty words

Terrify and persuade
As though true
The oil won't come off
My hands
Yes I thought of that too

How to become innocent
Enough
Which is of course again
To object to hunger
Simply

Because it is wrong
To assume that purity
Protects us
Is no good
Good until we free ourselves

xx.

Can loss be this
Organised

The nothing between
Us now

You but not you
Here but not as you were

First this and then this
Then this again

This no longer
Love we observe

These stanzas were written to be read in any order within each section. The present order was arranged by the editor.

NYLA MATUK

On Palaces

I may regret abandoning Norman O. Brown's *Love's Body*.
I was reading about patriarchy, the love and death drives,

the way Marx and Freud explained them and weaponized
such long chains of command, the civilizing discourse

against a *mission civilisatrice* that has excused the killing
of millions. I saw the boulevards lined with linden trees

designed with great zeal by that capricious actor
who applied himself with such fervour as the Marquise von O.'s

lover, his assurances that new projects were in
the offing, and, complete, proven highly successful.

Baudrillard claimed the horror of dying in the World Trade Center
towers no worse than having to go work in them every day.

The owners of the al-'Amawi Eastern and Western
Palaces demolished them during the British Mandate.

The Rabah Effendi al-Husayni Palace was turned into the American
Colony Hotel. The palace of Salim bin Husayn al-Husayni

became the Dar al-Tifl al-'Arabi, The House of Arab Children,
where the orphans of Deir Yassin, the only massacre documented

in *Time* magazine, came to live. Al-Mufti Tahir al-Husayni Palace,
established by the son of the Mufti of Jerusalem, became

a cultural venue. The Chairman of the Education Council
Isma'il Haqqi al-Husayni built the Orient House Palace

in 1897. It hosted Wilhelm II, Emperor of Germany and King of Prussia,
and his wife Augusta Victoria. It hosted King Abdullah

and Prince Zayd of Saudi Arabia, Haile Selassie, Emperor of Ethiopia,
and his wife Empress Menan, after their exile. It was the funeral site of many

martyrs of 1948. It was a hotel; it housed the United Nations
Relief Works Agency, then the Palestine Liberation Organization,

and was eventually pillaged by the occupier, of its 17,000 books
in both English and Arabic, dozens of periodicals, and the private

papers of Musa Al-'Alami; the documents of the Arab Higher
Committee, of the Palestinian army, *al-Jihad al-Muqaddas*, and others –

pictures and private notes, glass negatives of the Ottoman
period, and a fine collection of family photographs.

Dedicated to the memory of my elders who defended Sheikh Jarrah, Mahmoud alBakri and
Idris alBakri, freedom fighters and native sons of Jerusalem.

KRISZTINA TÓTH, *translated by Owen Good*

Time, Time, Time
for Judit Scherter

In my childhood at a relative's,
in the widowed, flannel-shirted forester's
poky flat, among his bulky furniture,
was a broken grandfather clock.
It was full of compartments,
making it seem mysterious,
purposeless, like the empty dovecote
in my classmate's yard.
It's timeless, said the grown-ups solemnly,
and as it hadn't worked for years, there was a dignity,
I thought, in the motionless hands. My parents
had wristwatches but never any time.
I longed for my own distant time, on the other side,
where one day I would have my own
timeless clock whose hands
were not to be touched.

There was always time to kill there.
I was bored. Browsing a hunting album on the floor,
the wide eyes of the rabbits and deer.
Time's not an easy kill.
Years go by before you learn how
to track time and get behind it.
Time lies heavy, dragging through the shady,
vast woodland of my life: its legs tied,
laid waste, I trail dead time
behind me, like a sledge.
They ask: what's that cord in the picture?
What's on the end of the rope, hanging
out of view? Nothing, I answer,
and they might ask who's that pulling.

That's me, I'd reply,
That's me all old.

Don't run out of time – I was forever told,
you'll never have a language certificate, a house, a child,
you'll miss the last bus, the greatest love,
you'll never be a ballet dancer, you'll never be a young mum,
or an old mum, for that matter, you can't run
through your life among all these people barefoot,
look at your feet, you've got those
girl's sandals on again, your buckles undone,
run after the others, quick!
I ran like the rabbits, like the deer,
eyes wide open, throbbing
ribs, sick to the stomach, in dreamed-of
Sunday shoes, always behind,
stumbling to the corner of the picture,
then looked up, it had got dark,
and I'd made it out of time.

SARALA ESTRUCH

Ghazal: Say
after Will Harris

There is *no definable point at which a living organism dies*, scientists say.
It shakes me to read words I've been striving all these years to find, to say.

The universe is rarely ordered in binary ways. How to articulate this
basic and profound truth my mind struggles to believe, let alone say?

All I know is you've been gone these long years and, at the same time, you haven't,
you've been right here, though, till now, it's not something I thought I could say.

'Dead' and 'alive' are terms *whose meanings are wholly psychological.*
Physiochemically [... they] merge into one another. They bleed, you could say.

Bleed the way my knee did, releasing its dark stain; running too fast to meet you
I fall, and what was once inside me now on your hands, your blue shirt. Sorry, I say.

You pull me close. In the garden beside the alley in which we crouch,
the chestnut trees are whispering, a sound only half got out. Sorry, you say.

The whispering grows louder, reverberates in my ear, my throat.
Father, and Poet. Tell me honestly. What are you – what am I – trying to say?

Italicised words are quotations from 'The Map of Four Kisses', an essay by Nuar Alsadir.

denial (i)

when she said the words   i didn't cry   didn't do anything

out of the ordinary   did i open my mouth   to speak

      i don't recall   & we continued

our walk   past the playground   the children

screaming   chasing   their ever-receding childhoods

at the bottom of the hill   we circled   two ponds

in the centre   the dark green water   choked

with algae   round & round   we went

small islands   only winged creatures   could reach

K PATRICK

Pickup truck sex

Awake early I look at this photo by Phyllis Christopher. I wish you could see it. Two strong people in white t-shirts fuck across the bonnet of an old pickup truck. One hand grips a wing mirror, the other pins a hip. A nipple is almost in a mouth. Fists are half formed. Two faces and their creases. Dawn comes in through my window, picking out the dust. Each face crease has a little history of its own. You have to make time for that, for each crease. Pleasure will continue to fold us up. (We are only pieces of paper.)

It is sunrise for me. For them I'm guessing it is afternoon. Bare thighs set sail across hot metal. Warm ear lobes, warm cheeks. Big knees like altars. The ability to be both bodies is my fantasy. Do you think that's arrogant? To at once wear the strap-on and feel it enter. In confessing this fantasy here I achieve another: writing strap-on in a poem. Elizabeth Freeman would label this "erotohistoriography". For example looking at this photo is important, therefore I am important. In the bedroom mirror I try to angle my knees to be more like altars.

I project onto the before. A small moment passes between these two bodies. They're walking to the truck. Not holding hands I don't think but wondering if they should. The afternoon sun leaves flowers wide open. Different insects are interrupted by skin. Like me maybe the first person is allergic to the plants in the field. A sneeze is perhaps the small moment. Tension broken temporarily, one smile, one more smile. No hand holding but an arm squeeze. Those beautiful wrist watches they consent to keep on.

In unison we thrive in transitory places. I am the small moment. Brief as a sneeze. More face creases: there can be future again. I'm not being as romantic as you think. What I've already said is I'd like to be fucked by myself. This isn't loneliness, but a coming together. I can feel the sun on my shoulders. A bee "rubs up against" my shin. What other way is there to be a sneeze in this photo? Out my window dawn is over. I'd perform well as a cloud in their sky.

Walk

When is a wood not a wood. She points out the cold pillboxes left behind by WW2. *Right now!* Slaps her hand against the concrete. *God loves a monument!* Fingers are an edgeland, in-between the body and otherwise. This is how she described me once: *inbetweeny.* A robin comes out strong. *Nothing here is original! Everything was planted for use!* Always speaking upwards that's her aim. I admire the robin's smooth body. She slaps the concrete again and smiles. We have the same teeth. Too soft, endless fillings. A pair of mouths full of chalk. These are Dad's lips though. Pillowy masculine energy; a decent smacking sound. Fussing over a yew tree she asks me to look up its leaves. "Ancient, morbid, toxic" I read the short blurb aloud. *Now that's masculine energy!* Her voice shuts up the robin. *Grow a pair!* She hisses at him in half meaning then latches onto my arm. Winter has carved us out. Two more silhouettes against the escarpment. *Who can resist an aside!* Moving on she mentions the masculine energy of other evergreen plants. Really she is talking about me, about my lips. *Narcissism runs in the family you see!* After the concrete she slaps the bark. Chalk is chunky through the soil too. Good enough to draw with. She chooses me a piece. *Go on!* But I can't touch that many skeletons at once

COLIN CHANNER

Lent

I mount a crest in coffee country and it's Oregon.
In all directions, ridges saw the Caribbean out of view.
In these wet mountains, clichés of the tourist

board elapse, beach fables die famished,
palms straggle, get left behind as pine and casuarinas
gather up in bamboo lushness with the blue mahoe.

I'm backpacked like a turtle, urgent-slow – flat-footed,
flippered in caricature, years after the surgery
and the knees just not the same, but why am I

sloshing fact with expectation – age is desiccating,
cartilage fails – and why confabulate? In this wet-air
ecotone before the clouds dismiss the fog and claim

the forest, green is dense as smoke. At this height,
the roads from Kingston show themselves:
escaped undressing runaways: tarmac, gravel, track,

and I sense ahead of me oblivion in the green-absorbing
white-gray silver, the clouds among the roots of trees
a shifting wisping thing. I'm elated and embarrassed.

Seeing relations of what ought to be disparate
is my living, my burden, my habit, my gift.
I left this island early, never learned to love with value

in my language, my fishes, my birds, my trees,
and as I do without my contacts, I see what's there
but not apparent, sense essence, trace travels,

overdubbing – map. In this way I'm kin to semi-literates,
brother to naives. Error-maker, I navigate on faith.
Small point: none of these trees are native. Like,

well, *me*, in the generic, they were brought. And as I
inch here in self-cloud wrapped in dense wetness that's actual,
glimpsing every now and then a farm – coffee bushes

with red dottings swerving with awareness
of the contour lines (said farm always well-terraced),
I imagine what it must have meant

to be a bringer, one gifted with the say to make a cut,
a shift, a graft, a cauter – suggesting by decree as interrogative:
"What if we bring *this* from there and make it grow *here*,

and transport it *thusly* so I can have more comfort in my
part-time home?" Mist, deep forest (and too much Walcott, frankly),
have a way of making poets fantasists (infantilists?) of exile.

I left is all, and swiftly. Now I know no birds by shape or color,
sound or season, silhouette or ceiling of flight, or what fruit
bears in what season, except in New England where I live.

What does this make me? I've never lived on the West Coast
much less Oregon, but I've been there, and those hills
I walked beyond Portland called me home to here,

these arabica mountains draped in mist, cloud covered
as though modest, where creeks occur as sound, pulling
me to Sahel travels, to courtyards marked by mud walls,

spume fountains; to heard-of women veiled. Here,
hip shapes form out of rustle, Kromanti women
ghost from shadow, ghillie-plumed a century plus

from patient self-erasure from the force of busha's pen;
here where slaves reconstituted, made war and news
by raids from hidden passage, from quick-effacing trail,

I know each aqua pool gyrates below the river's
urgent silver – blatant – but I don't. I understand the colonizer,
get the substandard with an inkling a promotion lay elsewhere

perhaps-feasibly-conceivably-perchance;
share the dubious heritage of gaze, of making all before me
what I want, gating my imagined, seeing me in everything,

accosting landscapes and handing them confessions,
making them my subjects, what I study, but in that childish style
(ask my profs at Hunter), without diligence, eliding grains,

compressing essence: touché Bennett: colonizing in reverse.
The remix is dub's premise. Reggae conquers. Not maybe actual.
But it's how it sees the world. There is more to say on this.

All I know is beyond these mountains is a Portland,
a whole parish with beaches in soft valleys classified
from day-trippers to the hills, banks of white sand umbrellaed

by ferns, cataracts with chromatic pools, slim and subtle falls.
A poet said and please don't quote me, that travelers
are the last arrivants – like soft waves they come with sorrows;

we regard them, then they come with conquest... you.
I am, and I am not. I accept this. But I don't.
I am that I am I am I am I am. This is Tosh.

Spear jooks: *My way is so long but the road is so foggy, foggy.*
Who am I to question these prophets, men who took the time
to know the names of trees and herbs, which fishes schooled

in what season, air pressure's augury – odd migrating of birds?

SHERI BENNING

Of

      the swineherd on the sovkhoz,
Arkhangelsk Oblast, who steals handfuls of corn
meant for hogs. Who forages the Soyanna's ravine
for nettles, sorrel, bear onion, club moss. Who at night
spoon-feeds her fevered sister earthen broth,
bunk window cataracted with steam.

Of
      the fevered sister who dreams
their father stands up from where he was shot. *Kulak!*
the commissar barked. *Run to the house*, Father says
in the dream, dusting chaff from his coat. *Tell Mama
I'll be in for supper soon.* Bloom of blood,
his burst heart, furls back into bud.

Of
      Oma who sings, *If I had a thousand hearts,
I'd give them all to you*, after they open the cattle cars,
give spades to the men to bury their dead by the tracks.
Stop! a man sobs. *Stop singing at once!* Oma's voice,
Maria zu lieben, murmuration of Black Sea
starlings, waves of wings dusk-bronzed.

Of
      the swineherd who holds her sister
in Arctic owl-light, a shawl of faint stars, listens
to White Sea wind. *When I die*, Oma said in the dark
car, *don't be sad – it means I found a way to trick Stalin.*
Cracked lips against vellus, she whispers Oma's song
in her sister's ear, *If flesh and hell battle,
you are my shelter.*

Of
      Mama in her daughter's typhoid-dream.
Look at this mess! She must tidy up, unknots the tablecloth,
loaves back in the cupboard, sweeps shards of china
into the corner. She tongue-clucks her youngest hiding
on the porch, *Your red apple cheeks!* She breathes
the clove of her girl's unwashed hair,
reties her scarf,

                there, there. You can't stay here;
    we are dead. Then she pushes her out,
leans all her weight against the door.

Ponteix, Saskatchewan: July 1929

Wilhelmina in a well, sour water
ankle high, a rope around her waist tied to the lip.
Mother leans in, her face, a moon, eclipses the glimpse
of blood-blister-blue noon sky – *If you fall, I'll pull*
you out as Wilhelmina climbs the ladder down,

down, down, 35 feet, to mop the spilled milk,
well-walls hung with butter and cream. At night,
Wilhelmina sleeps with her sisters in the steep attic,
a house of bleached bones. Bronchial tubes broken –
pneumonia-scarred lungs, she coughs,

coughs, coughs – I'll pull you out – wakes
into scabland. Cacti and sage, sandy loam, glacial wash,
constellations of stone. Spring wheat like lace, four bushels
an acre, salt grass and sulphate sloughs. But before
Mother shouts, before the tug of the rope,

she dreams cherry blossom drifts, rain's cricket-hiss,
wet oil of earth. She swears for the rest of her life that
when she looked up from the deep, she could see
Sirius, Vega, Venus or Mars. Of course,
she could not.

If she did not

wake in the night to her new sister's cry,
cracked seed, undone swaddling, husks
of their dead father's dream.

If she did not balm the baby's stiff belly
with mint and absinthe emulsified lard,
waxing crescent gleam in lamp-felted dark.

If she did not listen to Old Aunty
who said, *Let Mother rest.* Nine days in bed
for the bones to knit back. Poultice of thyme

so the womb will shed. Boil crocus,
rosehip and hyssop for cramps.
If you are scared, sing

"*Nightmare, nightmare, you cannot enter –*"
Mama's fast breath, brow hallowed
with sweat, the whites of her eyes,

moons shroud in high cirrus.
If you are scared, come find me. If she did not
slip out the door, beyond the skirt of porchlight

into snow-sifted shadow. If she did not lean against
ice-whetted wind, and when she heard the keen,
the tightening noose of wolves,

if she did not curl up on frozen furrows,
cover her face with her hood, small sips of air
melting the fresh skiff, wheat stubble, cold dirt,

the warm muzzle's nudge, uric steam –
Nightmare, nightmare, not until you've swum the seas,
not until you've crossed the field. If she did not

get up. If she did not keep walking to brushstrokes
on the horizon, their neighbour's copse,
poplar, willow, birch.

TAYLOR STRICKLAND

Lichen

Life is blemished and golden
moonglow, a lichen borne of love,
the fruiting body you did not become.
Or did you? We couldn't keep you
hidden in the tussocks of panic
forever, but when you kicked,
fifth instar to a shimmering
green, you were still our little secret.
You quickened into life and through
your mother as she began to darken
with the days: hips to belly button
enclosed a faint line, smile mottled,
a mask cracked into mosaic,
and all during the first trimester.
Too early. I said we're too young.
Never said I was
afraid, but I was. So afraid
I couldn't hear what your mother was
afraid of, this being her one chance.
I didn't see, didn't see
behind surfaces of lichen-grey
overgrowing everything
what you were meant to be: summer's
day-flying butterfly, our mountain ringlet,
rare in your desire for montane air.
Instead you were turned to script lichen,
forked, curved letters no one would believe,
not even me. When the floor
revealed you were bloodspot lichen
I knew what I had done.
Even now, six years since your mother and I
rinsed our fingers clean, I still liken you

to chrysalis, a black word. Black after green,
after regret. The wound death brings
is the afterlife.

Heil Valley
for David George Haskell

Field run to seed along the grain
of granite, trees under dusk and ruin
complete any piecemeal dark.
Blacker than char, a squirrel angles
toward pitched meadowland, listens
for anything else, an owl
concealed by shadow, or far off,
fast through the canyon that never stops,
the wind-splitter, a motorcycle
dying into night. Nature's sonographer
with big probing ears, it can read sound
as well as hear. Watch how it scans
woodsmoke for a seasonless year
high among the pine-fork, then re-builds
its needle-stitched cup, cache that was
brimful with seed, berry and acorn,
until it realizes nothing
discerns nothing after wildfire, after
the aftermath. Only loss, and worse
the evergreen of memory is reversed
to never-green, a nothing-nest,
so eerily similar to nothingness.

POLLY ATKIN

Mast Year / Helplessness Subscale

beech shells falling a storm of them sheeting
down siling down it is terrible
and I think it is never going to get any better
plut plut plut plut on the cobbles huge
rippling drops falling to a swelling
flood sinking into the mud then welling
out of the mud it is awful and I feel
that it overwhelms me the ground throwing
them up as the branches throw them down
the lane drowned under the sudden river
washed clean of itself I worry all the time
about whether the pain will end and they
become the lane and the lane crunches
under your feet I feel I cannot
stand it any more with each
step into winter I feel I cannot
go on which might last seven years
which you may emerge from altered owing
some kind of tithe there is nothing I can do
to reduce the intensity of the pain

Gravitas / Rumination Subscale

Every point mass attracts every single
other point mass by a force acting
along the line intersecting – can I keep
on falling interminably? – the force is proportional
to the product of the masses and inversely proportioned
to the square of the distance between them. The sound
that falls from my mouth like a plumb line when my knee
hits the ground. The crack of a thin bone placed
under pressure from the right direction or slap
of palm on ice. This is the law.
I anxiously want. I anxiously want.
I am a point mass falling, blood
sloshing down the slouching stocking of a body
any time I let it act on me, inciting it
by standing, invoking it any time I rise.
I cannot seem to keep it out of my mind. Are we
going to rise up? And fall down again, sickened
and dizzy with the dream of rebellion, counter
the tyranny of downward motion. Of the planet's
dense core. I keep thinking about how badly I want.
This is the relationship between the motion of the moon
and the motion of a body falling. If the bodies
in question have spatial extent. If the bodies
are in question. If the bodies have attraction as all
massive bodies must do, for each other, for the sky
and the centre. It is unavoidable. I keep thinking
how badly I want the pain to stop.
I anxiously. I catastrophically. I
massively. I subject to scalar gravity. I
stand and let go. I kiss the earth.
This is serious.
I keep thinking about how much it hurts.

'GBENGA ADEOBA

Tableau

I do not know how it became frayed
or shed its gleam, but in this photograph
I am two, standing behind my grandmother's window,
in a yard between the main house and her quarters,
where an unknown kid left evidence of their numerical
skills on the wall. The gold necklace on my neck slants
slightly to the left, betraying the body's posture.
Downwards, in this image of an image, I see,
when I zoom in, a cicatrix had made its home
on my left knee. My mother says
my grandmother was there beside her,
urging me to drop my folded arms to my side,
unburdened – the grace of a bird
yielding itself to the winds.

20 Gbogi Street (Revisited)

The little I know of houses
I learned from the rain
   – John Burnside

I greet the old woman
at the door, answer her inquiry
of the weather. She had kept

some rods to drive the goats
who linger here, but she calls
out to her daughter-in-law

to herd them in. Some large
and heavy, the goats trudge
through the lit passage

as one might in high snow,
past the younger woman
counting the lot, nodding

now as she always does
when they are complete; her face
aglow as she latches the gate.

Essay

ON THE BONE

Natalya Anderson

Across the spectrum of their careers, the choreographer Twyla Tharp and the poet Sharon Olds have shared a likeness in the way they have documented the female ageing process. Through dance and lyric, Tharp and Olds have created maps of their bodies at transition points in their lives, exploring such experiences as sex, pregnancy, divorce, illness, and physical deterioration beyond middle age. Where Tharp describes her work as "the only way out" of the mental distress that ageing brings for her, Olds appears to write herself into the process of physical change as a coping device. Both artists describe their work as "useful lessons" on what the body and mind are capable of. In keeping with their particular artforms, they approach their material from different directions. Dance has historically been a discipline that works outward and then within – the methodology of training involving a personal relationship with the mirror, from which established dancers and choreographers can migrate inward with emotional expression once their classical training has been embedded in their physicality. Poetry does a resistance dance of its own, but often begins with deeply personal material around which form has to be scaffolded and structured. But while Tharp may be choreographing outward as Olds is folding herself in, reflecting the nature of their forms, both are maintaining "an alliance with death", dancing through each year in order to teach themselves and others about what it means to survive.

Twyla Tharp explained in a recent *New York Times* interview that she consumes no more than 1,200 calories a day, as part of her survival method. "It's a little crazy," she acknowledges. "But it helps me keep myself on the bone, which is important, because the less weight I put onto feet, the better off we are." After the age of sixty-five, she says (she is now eighty years old), "I got nothing for free. I had to work hard for every little thing, and that could be discouraging, to say the least. So how to maximize that? How do we learn from some of these newer moves that the body comes up with just to survive?"

While she was pregnant, Tharp retreated to the attic in her home and recorded herself dancing a series of steps. She repeated this daily throughout the pregnancy to document how her dancing changed as her body changed. "So, how does a body change?" Tharp asks in the PBS documentary *Twyla Moves*. "This was going to be an opportunity to learn some interesting lessons. There was no other way to do it." In describing her work, Tharp frequently refers to there being "no other way" than following a particular practice, or that it is "the only way out". It's as if, as in the example of her pregnancy project, she is scrutinising the body not so much to escape this physical phase in her life, but rather in order to coexist with its precariousness. Although she makes it clear now that she does not enjoy ageing ("What do you think? What's to reflect? It sucks"), Tharp simultaneously works to live in harmony with the process. So while she wants out, she continues to seek artistic use from getting older.

Dance historian Maura Keefe views Tharp's method from this perspective: "This is typical dancemaking by Tharp: at the same time as she is deeply involved in the kinesthetics of the actions, she is also coolly analytical in her observation of the evolving form of each dance from the outside." Keefe's observations apply not only to Tharp's work, but also to the very nature of dance as a discipline. Dancers are taught in front of a wall of mirrors, and their relationship with the mirror is a step up from their first initiation into studio life, which involves a very physical audition. The dancer learns from childhood that outward appearance and alignment are key to how they will match other dancers in a company. The mirror becomes second-in-command to their teacher as a silent disciplinarian – a relationship that is not often spoken about in the dance world. It makes sense therefore, that Tharp, who also filmed her earliest work, might continue to work outward and then access the emotional core of her work from that outside focal point.

Sharon Olds, who will be seventy-nine this year, is also deeply invested in manifesting the body and its experiences in her work. Like Tharp, she wants her art to serve a purpose ("I want a poem to be useful", she has commented). Where Tharp analyses from the outside, Olds documents her own physicality from within, writing herself into parts of her body, or merging with another's. In contrast with dance, we might think of poetry as a more internal, cerebral practice, which works from the inside out, rather than the outside in. A poet may resist this process, just as a dancer might struggle with the resistance of her body. As Mary Ruefle writes in her lecture 'On Secrets' (2012), "Poems are written in secret. [...] The two sides of a secret are repression and expression, just as the two sides of the poem are the told and the untold."

An early example of Olds working with this push-pull between the emotional and the physical can be seen in her poem 'First' (from her 1996 collection *The Wellspring*), in which she details a first experience of oral sex. This encounter is not depicted from an observational point of view; rather it is presented as a kind of nourishing, healing act for the speaker's own body:

> I was a sophomore
> at college, in the baths with a naked man,
> a writer, married, a father, widowed,
> remarried, separated, unreadable, and when I
> said No, I was sorry, I couldn't,
> he had invented this, rising and dripping
> in the heavy sodium water, giving me his body to suck. I had
>   not heard
> of this, I was moved by his innocence and daring,
> I went to him like a baby who's been crying
> for hours for milk.

In a *New Yorker* interview with the poet, journalist Alexandra Schwartz suggests these early depictions of sex in the poems are ways that Olds testifies and heals after trauma. Olds has spoken at length about her upbringing in an abusive, Calvinist home in which sex was a taboo topic and yet her body was frequently stripped naked to be beaten by her mother. In her analysis of 'First', Schwartz proposes that the poem gives the author permission to explore her body:

> Sex was the first means of healing. Olds frequently borrows religious tropes to write of her erotic life, letting the body take the place where religion had been [...]. Later in "First," Olds compares the innate body knowledge awakened in her in the sulfur pool to the experience of rubbing her mother's back, "receiving directions from her want into the nerves of my hands." This taboo trespassing, the crossing of family with sex, is typical of Olds. The intent is not to provoke, but to testify.

This desire to testify continues in the work of both Tharp and Olds as they age. In her poem '35/10', which first appeared in 1982, Olds compares herself, at the age of thirty-five, to her ten-year-old daughter. Here, again, she writes herself very intimately into the body of the poem, almost imagining herself as her daughter as she grapples with the idea of her own physical change:

> As my skin shows
> its dry pitting, she opens like a small
> pale flower on the tip of a cactus;
> as my last chances to bear a child
> are falling through my body, the duds among them,
> her full purse of eggs, gold and
> firm as hard-boiled yolks, is about
> to snap its clasp. I brush her tangled
> fragrant hair at bedtime. It's an old
> story—the oldest we have on our planet—
> the story of replacement.

Here the speaker is mapping herself onto another person's body; where previously she wrote herself into a healing sexual process, which she sought to transfer to her mother through touch, here the possession and transference involves her daughter, as if this work might facilitate an acceptance or overcoming of the ageing process. Kate Kellaway has suggested that this tactic might be Olds's way of forming a kind of friendship with physical decline, in order to surmount the emotional distress ageing brings. Here is where Olds's poems, like Tharp's choreography, continue to be "useful" lessons. "There is self-petitioning: she will unthink her thoughts, she will praise, accept and attempt to love," Kellaway writes in a review of Olds's 2016 collection *Odes*. "Not that any of this is comfortable. Imagining herself as 'hardly human' is shocking. She writes about age's alliance to death – just one of the taboos she breaks – with a driven perkiness [...] Sharon Olds once told me she wanted her poems to be 'useful'. These odes, because they illuminate what it is to live inside a body and survive its outrages, are useful – and beautiful too."

Olds also creates this useful beauty in her Pulitzer Prize-winning collection *Stag's Leap* (2012), in which she documents the events leading up to her divorce and her experience, as she later describes it in *Odes*, of being "a fresh left / wife" ('Ode to Whiskers'). Critics of the collection praised Olds for her "lack of anger" in the poems, missing the opportunity to see the deep, inward motion of her writing, particularly when she, once again, seeks to fold herself entirely into a body part as it ages. Consider the opening of her 'Poem for the Breasts':

> Like other identical twins, they can be
> better told apart in adulthood.
> One is fast to wrinkle her brow,
> her brain, her quick intelligence. The other
> dreams inside a constellation,
> freckles of Orion. They were born when I was thirteen,
> they rose up, half out of my chest,
> now they're forty, wise, generous.
> I am inside them—

Irrespective of the poet's relationship with anger, which is beside the point, Olds demonstrates here the ways in which she uses her ageing body during times of strife to teach herself something about survival. In a conversation about *Stag's Leap* with journalist Sabine Durrant, Olds discusses a kind of self-teaching that has become intertwined with her poetry: "During our conversation she refers to various things she had to learn for herself", writes Durrant:

> Loyalty: 'One picks it up by imitation and if, as in my case, you are never shown it as a child, you can have difficulties learning it.' Motherhood: 'I understood so little about it. In expressing, we slowly come to understand a little more.' Anger: 'If you grow up thinking anger is a danger to the soul, that it is not an option, it takes a while to know how to get appropriately angry, to respect your own emotions.'

Olds suggests that this kind of deep physical examination might be linked to the process of composition, which, in turn, allows for lessons in healing: "I focus so hard on the line, like a gladiator in the arena with the lions, just trying to be accurate, not being gloomy about your condition, but making something which may prove to be good."

It is worth noting that while Tharp and Olds work in different disciplines as they examine the female body, Tharp is in some ways a poet, and Olds is very much a dancer. Consider how Tharp, when pushed by a news broadcaster to describe how she choreographed her breakthrough piece 'Eight Jelly Rolls' in 1971, describes the dance moves of one microcosm in the dance:

> There are some very literal gestures. I mean, for example, the banjo solo that I do starts out with "Hitching a ride down the street. How do you do? I'm knocking off my foot. Oh, yeah, there it goes. Oh, I see it. I see it. I still need a ride. How are you? I'm washing my hands of this whole mess. Oh, I hate you a lot. I'm bowing down here, this cello. I am shooting craps. Shame on you. You're a bad person. Traffic goes this way. Hello out there. Again, I will polish the mirror, and then bouncing a basketball. And this is my motion of some Jewish something or other. And then we have this black bottom number put in, because it is called The Black Bottom Stomp. And then we go to the knock-

kneed sheriff, and the last little dirty movement that we can put
in before it comes to fast diagonal." And that all happens at this
tempo [*claps hands three times*].

One might compare Tharp's description of her choreography to a
Rosemary Tonks poem. Olds, meanwhile, when asked about her craft in
an interview for *The Moth* in 2020, delivers a downright balletic response:

> I've certainly had a passionate relationship with craft. It's a little
> like improv rock and roll. I did ballet as a child and then at 15,
> Fats Domino started singing 'Blueberry Hill' and I was at a junior
> high and there were kids there who were dancing so expressively,
> and I asked someone how did they learn that, and he said, 'You
> just do what you want.' So I just started dancing. And that would
> not have been recognizable in ballet terms or dancing school
> terms. I was dancing with it and then against it, in counterpoint
> to it, and I love that. I love that so much.

Olds illustrates this relationship in a very physical manner in a 2011
Poets.org panel discussion available on YouTube, 'Breaking the Line,
Breaking the Narrative'. When asked how she approaches line breaks,
she stands up, begins a series of airy, willowy gestures with her back
and arms, and offers this reply: "It's like a pine tree, kind of, or a
hemlock. Over here is the mirror of that, which is not in language and
is not written, but is like the life, that the spirit, that this matter of
language is representing, in a way. The whole thing, also, has a sense to
me of a dervish dance."

Just as Olds transfers between dance, music, and lyric in her writing,
Tharp also came to transfer easily between her more traditional classical
training and contemporary experimentation in choreography and music.
She has long paired classical dance with rock and roll, or modern
choreography with classical music. The idea of marrying young and old
is something Tharp has played with since she created her 1973 piece
'Deuce Coup' for the Joffrey Ballet, with classically trained dancers
performing to music by The Beach Boys. She interchanges this process
repeatedly during her career, with classical and modern meshing in
celebrated choreographic works like 'Push Comes to Shove' (1976), 'In

the Upper Room' (1986), 'The Brahms Haydn Variations' (2000), and countless others.

One of Tharp's most fascinating experiments with meshing old and new is 'The Catherine Wheel', created in 1981 when Tharp was forty. Inspired by the legend of St Catherine, a fourth-century martyr who aimed to achieve spiritual perfection by overcoming her human failings, this piece was revolutionary in 1981, as Tharp combined technology with dance, all to the music of Talking Heads' David Byrne. Catherine is depicted in a non-human electronic form. Her human counterpart, Sara, is doomed to fail in her attempt to achieve the discipline and physical control of the computerised Catherine. Tharp explores the body from the outside, with a computerised woman superimposed onto a real one. One can see the female version of da Vinci's Vitruvian Man, arms and legs stretched out in a wheel for perpetual scrutiny.

"When 'The Catherine Wheel' began," Twyla remarks in *Twyla Moves*, "it started with the idea that technology could offer a new look at a dancer. 'The Catherine Wheel' has one of the first motion-capture figures. And it has some sort of video experiments that certainly helped me with the foundation for what we're trying to do in the Zoom stuff." The "Zoom stuff" she refers to is one of her latest pieces, choreographed remotely during the pandemic, with dancers from around the world. Another testament to her desire to see what is possible in an impossible time, both physically as she approached eighty, and geographically with dancers beaming in via the internet, Tharp has created an online adaptation of her work 'The Princess and the Goblin', teaching dancers in their thirties choreography from her studio in New York.

"[Y]ou build up your backlog of experiences and lessons so that you get to be a certain age, and *then* you're ready to start", she tells the *New Yorker* when asked about ageing and whether she's evolved into a "new" choreographer as an older person:

> You're ready to get going because you might know something
> [...] And I think that it becomes more difficult as one ages, to
> have that kind of grasp and faith that you actually can find a new
> beginning. I mean, that's one of the things that obviously is so
> moving about Matisse. He was basically completely debilitated
> when he was able to make those massive breakthroughs with

the cutouts. It's that the physical destruction only tempers the spirit. And, also, the necessity to work – you don't put together a lifetime of information like this and walk away from it.

There is no walking away for Olds either, and the lifetime of work she has built as a poet provides ballast to her fearless examination of the ageing female body in *Odes*. With poems such as 'Ode of Withered Cleavage', Olds continues to walk straight into the body as it wrinkles, and she continues to surprise the reader by projecting onto and somewhat burrowing into another person's body. This time, again, it's her mother's. The second part of 'Ode of Withered Cleavage' moves from a description of her elderly mother's cleavage and the desire for touch, to the speaker's own desire to disappear, to become so aligned with the ageing process that she could be unrecognisably old:

> My mother's desire to be touched,
> late in her life, was so intense I could
> almost hear it, like a keening from the hundred little
> purselets of each nipple, each like a
> rose-red eraser come alive and starvacious.
> And now my own declivity is
> arroyoing, and if I live long enough
> my chest over my breastbone may look like
> an internal organ, a heart trailing its
> arteries and veins. I want to praise
> what goes one way, what never recovers.
> I want to live to an age when I look
> hardly human, I want to love them
> equally, birth and its daughter and
> mother, death.

Here Olds writes herself into birth, motherhood, death, and rebirth, all in one sweeping poem. That useful beauty that Kellaway writes about is present toward the end of Schwartz's interview with Olds, and the peaceful strength with which Olds approaches writing seems on display even as she is taking a walk with the journalist:

As we walked together, Olds limped, the result of arthritis. She wasn't in pain, she said, just slowed down. In "Unmatching Legs Ode," she acknowledges that she is not so happy about the state of the soles of her feet, those "two brains, reading the ground" now missing half their nerves and rendered "numbskulls." But she still takes pleasure in her odd-couple legs, the left looking shrunken next to the swollen right [...] She thinks of her legs as "best friends," of hers and of each other. It's hard to imagine that the time will come to give them up.

"I'm sad they will rot", Olds writes in 'Unmatching Legs Ode'. "I wish our bodies / could leave us when they are done with us— / leave our spirits here, and walk away."

Whether choreographing as an outward analysis or writing introspectively, Tharp and Olds undoubtedly share a capacity and desire to detail the development of the female body over a lifetime. This desire is not, however, quite the same as the vanity of the artist who composes a paper and pencil compass to paint and sculpt from a perfected blueprint. Rather, Tharp and Olds have lived out a different kind of bodily mapping for entirely different purposes. Throughout impactful moments in a female body's life, Tharp and Olds have been parallel in their need to find answers for living life by leaning towards death. Tharp has recorded her body to calculate what it can do in each transitional phase of its existence. Her tendency to analyse from outside is likely due to her training in front of the mirror from a childhood reared in dance, and the personal scrutiny she continued to apply through filming herself in her attic, and choreographing works like 'The Catherine Wheel'. Olds, meanwhile, has often sought to embody others even as she writes of the experiences of her body, looking out from within in order to heal or baptise her own flesh anew, in a forever-dance of resistance in which secrets are released but somehow remain secrets through the coding of poems. If both artists are, indeed, looking in different directions during this process, it can be argued that they are also pledging an allegiance to death for themselves and others to learn from in a mission to survive their bodily deterioration, no matter how close they come to the bone.

Essay

OF MANY VOICES: A POETIC GIFT OF TOGETHERNESS

With a poem by Momtaza Mehri

Karen Simecek

In her collection of essays *About Poems*, Anne Stevenson casts lyric poetry as poetry of the voice and the ear. At first glance, we might interpret this as the singular voice of the poet and the ear of the reader. But poetry isn't so simple. In writing, some poets invoke other voices, sometimes fictional or constructed. In other cases, the voices they invoke are the real-life voices of others by incorporating words spoken and stories told into their work. Examples such as Brendan Kennelly's *Cromwell* and Carol Ann Duffy's *The World's Wife* show how the voices of historical figures can be brought to life through poetic representation. And then there are poems that aim to bring together the voices of others, voices that had been marginalised and left unheard in society. For instance, Charles Reznikoff's *Testimony: The United States (1885–1915): Recitative*, for which he draws on over five hundred court cases as source material. Through this long poem, Reznikoff presents the stories of many whose voices would have otherwise been lost to vast legal archives. Will Harris's 'The Crick' (2021) commissioned by Poet in the City for their project 'A Drop of Hope: Poetry from a Vaccination Centre' offers a more contemporary example of a poem that seeks to bring together the voices of others. Here's a brief extract:

> Four cabs, that's
> how many I tried
> to flag down
> to get here. Don't
> know how they
> knew. Was it
> my hair? My skin
> tone? I wore shades
> to hide my eyes.
> A snow moon
> hung over London
> as I travelled
> home. It looked
> like I felt.

Harris used the words visitors had written on postcards at the Francis Crick Institute during the UK's Covid-19 vaccination programme, as well as those of a volunteer he interviewed there. In an artist statement, Harris writes, "I decided to keep to the language of the responses, only altering personal pronouns and syntax where appropriate. I wanted the multiple voices to come together of their own accord, expressing the simultaneous anger, grief and hope of this moment." What's especially notable here is the poet's desire to bring multiple voices together unmodified; his aspiration, to allow the voices of others to find ways of connecting organically, resulting in a work that is truly multivocal.

Such poems have been called "poetic transcription", or "research poems", to capture a method of writing in which the poet uses interviews or other first-person accounts in the construction of their poem. As we will see, neither term quite represents what's going on in the writing of them. The poem may be wholly constituted by the words of others or added to/modified by the poet. This approach to writing can be traced to the centos (or patchwork poems) of ancient Rome, poems composed of lines from other poems. A modern example is John Ashbery's 'To a Waterfowl', in which he incorporates lines from Shakespeare, Hopkins, Eliot, Yeats, Browning, and Tennyson. Another reference point for poetic transcription can be located in the found poetry or "readymades" of Dadaism, such as Howard Nemerov's 'Found Poem'.

One might be tempted to think that all poetry involves some transcription of other voices. In outlining his method of cut-out poetry, William S. Burroughs famously declared all writing a "collage of words read and heard and overheard". Many poets draw on other voices in their work, taking inspiration from conversations, overhearings, and other encounters with language, but poetic transcription is more direct in its incorporation of other voices. Found poetry and other kinds of collage poetry are not necessarily sensitive to the origins of their material, appropriating words and phrases as mere resources for the poem. Such an approach doesn't address the situatedness of the original authors of those words, whether they belong to people who have been unjustly marginalised (due to ableism, homophobia, racism, sexism, etc) and whether appropriating their words causes further harm by removing context and changing meaning (thereby denying them a voice). Poetic transcription, on the other hand, aims to invoke the voices of others in addition to using their words and in doing so hopes to enable other voices to be heard and create community through poetry. It is therefore responsive to the ethics of who speaks and who gets to be heard (even if not always successful in meeting these ethical demands).

By 'voice' in poetry we often mean written words 'sounded' by (or presented to) the mind, rather than literally heard. In *About Poems*, Anne Stevenson draws a helpful distinction:

> There is the physical voice, an *articulation*, either vocal or mental – a pattern of long or short, stressed or unstressed syllables as they come to mind in the course of writing a poem. Then there is a sense in which the phrase 'the poet's voice' is used metaphorically to refer to an individual's speech idiom or characteristic mode of expression.

Although distinct, these two senses of poet's voice are connected, for the physical (or embodied) voice – which can be characterised in terms of one's imagined speech or the felt quality of language for some individuals – shapes the expressive voice, which is to do with how one uses language to share some aspect of thought, feeling or experience. The first grounds and centres language as embodied, that is, the sounds of words (albeit imagined or spoken aloud) are heard as located at a particular time and place. However, it is important to note that D/deaf poets may have a different understanding of voice. As John Lee Clark writes "Sound is only one of many vehicles through which poetry can travel from feeling and thought to expression and understanding. In other words, sound is mere medium, not source." In light of this, we can understand the physical voice as the existential voice: it presents the use of (written) language as the product of someone's thinking, feeling, and experiencing. The expressive voice is suggestive of intention and meaning; a desire to communicate. What is of interest here is not the 'voice of the poet' as such, which we might associate with questions of style and artistic vision, or the voice of a given reader, but rather voice understood as representative of a perspective. That is, the unique ways individual people see, think, and feel as manifest in their use and appreciation of language. In other words, how individual people use language and what they express through the language they use.

The possibility of a multivocal poetic, such as poems produced through the method of poetic transcription, raises questions about the relationship of the voice of the poet to the voices and voicings within their work. For instance, it's not clear whether the poet's voice is neutral in respect to other voices brought into the lyric fold or whether the poet's perspective dominates in the poem. If it's the case that even in a multivocal poem the poet's perspective dominates, then the ethical issue of who gets to speak and who gets to be heard returns. It's also not clear to what extent we should think of poetry as multivocal: does this apply to a very small number of poems or should this idea be applied to poetry at large? The following poem by Momtaza Mehri is not only a meditation on the role of voice in poetry but was written as "poetic minutes" of a discussion involving poets and members of the public on the nature of voice and voices in poetry in relation to another of Poet in the City's projects, 'Connected Through the Unknown: A Hounslow Covid Archive' (2020). The poem captures the response of the poet to the discussion together with traces of the voices of others who took part.

Momtaza Mehri
A Common Gift

Against vanity, I try to translate this philosophy of flight,
Of time's trickling pace, the race of words catching up to intentions.
Even the bearing of witness has its limits, its gated horizons.
Bare the wound's wonders. The sparrow-sized ball of delight
Buried in the chest. Is the poet a ventriloquist of the senses?
Who buries what has been unearthed?
Lives swallowed into the fold of verses. Each voice a shard
Of glass, uniquely jagged. An intricate lattice
Of particular joys & defeats.
How to give life to the stubborn beauty of difference?
Mine the depths of the ordinary. The poet tries.
Knows there is no such thing as ordinary.
Between storyteller & subject,
Boundaries disintegrate, between what is felt & what is transcribed.
Affinity is a group activity.
Attention binds the gap.
Generous exchange of details, of entangled paths, this slow dance
Of capturing the fleeting & often forgotten.
Be with each other, the poet said. The *with* is its own expanse,
A looping orbit
Of familiar ties. My story is his, hers, theirs, *ours*.
Craft a rearticulation of raindrops gracing the cheek,
A tea-stained book, the blossom
Of violets, the roar of planes overhead.
You don't have to experience something to understand it.
To preserve it in the cocoon of words is to illuminate
Some essential truth. To give it another, longer life that can
Be held in the lap
Of someone else. Nesting.

What is the role of the poet in relation to the voices they bring together? Mehri's poem works through the possibilities: bearer, translator, witness, ventriloquist, miner, burier, storyteller, transcriber, (re)articulator, preserver and (be)holder. None of these roles quite captures what the poet does. Rather than dwelling on the particularities of these roles, we can look to what they share: each represents a relationship between the poet and others. Rather than understanding poetry in terms of the singular voice of the poet, poetry can be seen as relational in the way it connects voices, including the poet's own.

Poet and literary critic Susan Stewart points to the relational aspect of sound and voice in lyric poetry in her book *Poetry and the Fate of the Senses* (2002). She writes:

> When we invoke or call for sound, we bring ourselves, too, into a certain path: we take our place in time. And when we attribute sound to a voice, we wonder what figure will be made, who speaks and from where – when the voice arrives, we learn something, too, about where we stand. Sound and voice in lyric [...] take part in these common aspects of aurality and the reception of aurality. Yet lyric also is made from silence, from the pull of sound against sense, and from places where voices are at the brink of their individuality. Such voices are filled with the voices of others who have been brought to bear on the speaking or singing person. The person is the vessel of the particular meeting of these particular voices.

If we think of the poet as voicing, or as a "vessel", of other voices we open up an understanding of poetry as a meeting place of voices. An intimate meeting place where voices can intersect and shape one another through the poet's voicing of words in the poem. "*Be with each other*" Mehri writes. Poetry offers a way of being together, that is, an empathetic connecting of others by experiencing and feeling together: poet to reader; voice to voice; voice(s) to reader; reader to reader. The "being with" signalling a form of contentment in the companionship of others, not a claiming of the other but sharing with another or others. Public language, by its very nature, is a way of being with others. In speaking, we use the words of others, not as belonging to them but as shared with them. We voice words that have been used by people before us and will be used again. Being users of language ties people together but also offers opportunity to influence others' use of language. Modifications of articulation (changing how a word is said) or meaning (changing its use) by an individual might be adopted by others, thereby shaping their use of language (sometimes this occurs at a cultural level but can also just happen between friends and smaller communities). Our physical voice is shaped by those we have communed with in our lives. It represents an intimacy with others who shape the ways we speak from the patterns of speech (and aurality of language) to the syntax and grammar of one's expression. Therefore, even the supposed univocal poem invokes multiple voices through the poet's singular voice. The poems I have been concerned with here, however, are doing this in a more explicit way – writing with intention about the relationship between voices (including historical voices that have shaped our own use of and sounding of language), how voices connect and how they might shape one another.

To bring multiple voices together, not only must the poet select elements that are shareable in terms of the physical voice, but the poet must also be able to 'sound' or 'give voice to' the other voices. The poet's task is to discover commonality with the patterns and rhythms of the other voices and their own. Other voices must be resonant with the poet's own for the poet cannot escape their own voice but can bring others together with or through it. In doing so, the poet must attend to, or rather, tend to, these other voices and the separation between them. Finding connections in rhythm and the aesthetics of language (such as assonance, consonance, and other aspects of the experiential beauty of the aurality of words) serves as the connecting force between voices, whilst allowing the voices to express difference in perspective. This is to disagree with philosopher and literary critic Mikhail Bakhtin who argues that the rhythmic structure of poetry "destroys in embryo those social worlds of speech and of persons that are potentially embedded in the word: in any case, rhythm puts definite limits on them, does not let them unfold or materialize." Instead, what the practice of bringing voices together achieves is to show us as part of the same social world by revealing ourselves as sharing in the expressive power of language. As Robert Pinsky writes "In a poem, the social realm is invoked with a special intimacy at the barely voluntary level of voice itself. Communal life, whether explicitly included or not, is present implicitly in the cadences and syntax of language: a somatic ghost." Poetry brings awareness of our intimacy with others through our use of language, that is, as members of a shared social and linguistic world (although this isn't necessarily inclusive, for instance, poetry that emphasises language as heard may exclude those who cannot hear).

Mehri's poem is structured so as to make present the joining of voices – the joining, or rather, conjoining of language. Many of its lines bring together two sentences, the full stop lying in the middle. A full stop that signifies a meeting place, a meeting of difference, different lives, different perspectives. The form reflects the fragmented nature of voice in the poem, making visible the rejection of singularity of voice. Each unit gives the possibility of its own history and perspective. The bringing together of voice is intimate, affective and bodily: these voices take on a felt connection to the poet's presence of 'being there', which is itself responsive in feeling. The voices of others are transfigured and united through the embodied voice of the poet, that is, by the poet's affective shaping through the act of vocalising other voices. This makes the poet's project harder for there is the need to preserve the individuality of each contribution yet in bringing them together the poet faces "the stubborn beauty of difference". If what is valued is difference, how does the poet bring these disparate voices together as one? How do voices meet in difference and yet remain sensitive to that difference?

There are many ways of invoking other voices. Voicing is something that can be done in the singular or plural. For instance, 'speaking for' or 'on behalf of' others is to bring voices together as one. When one is 'speaking on behalf of', the voices of the many are subsumed into the singular, dominant voice and consequently, the many are denied a continuing, active voice. However, on a plural conception of voicing, one speaks with others, allowing voices to speak on their own terms. Rather than 'speaking on behalf of' others, the poet takes on the role of democratic representation by allowing the poem to be dynamic in its voices and voicings – letting other voices shape the poet's own as it figures in the poem. However, poetry can never be a mere collage of other voices. The poet must weave these voices together and in the process re-shape and re-voice the words from the community. What results is a mutual re-shaping of voice. In such a poem, the poet speaks "against vanity" for their voice is not privileged in the poem; the poet does not claim to be all knowing or have some special access to truth. The poet's 'gift' is in their ability to bring (both historically and geographically distinct) voices together in companionship to present something greater than the individual self. Such multivocal poetry brings voices into a relationship through the lyric and in doing so, allows the poem to express a collective, human perspective from what is shared between: "Lives swallowed into the fold of verses. Each voice a shard / Of glass, uniquely jagged. An intricate lattice / Of particular joys & defeats". The image of the shards of glass represents the many voices invoked in poetry as mimetic reflections, aspects, glimmers of voice through the words, phrases, meanings, and patterns of speech. What is captured in the work is only ever partial and incomplete. The voices that are expressive of individual lives figure in the poem as shards of glass, incomplete, removed from the whole and unable to be fitted back into place. Something of the other remains in the poem but much is lost. In drawing on other voices, the poet does not remove the relationship to other voices; a trace of another always remains. What is lost is gained in the emergence of a social and relational plurality that embodies what brings voices together.

> To preserve it in the cocoon of words is to illuminate
> Some essential truth. To give it another, longer life that can
> Be held in the lap
> Of someone else. Nesting.

Mehri presents poetry as a nesting of voices: within one's voice are the traces of others. Embedded. How we speak, how we structure our sentences, choose our words are all the product of the influence of others. This is how we preserve one another's ways of seeing the world in our language. The poet's nesting of other voices within the voice of the poem also nourishes and nurtures those other ways of thinking, feeling, and experiencing for it will hold them until they take flight amongst the breath of readers and ears of listeners.

UP ALL NIGHT

Jack Underwood, Not Even This: Poetry, Parenthood and Living Uncertainly, *Corsair, £14.99,* ISBN 9781472156082

Stephanie Burt on a poet's prose study of fatherhood

. . .

When our younger child was about five months old, they insisted (as far as we could tell) on sleeping in the same bed as myself and my partner. They were still nursing. They were tiny, and tiny humans deserve cuddles. So I contorted myself, night after night, and fell asleep beside two lovely humans, one adult and one very far from it, and woke up curled, achy and awkward, and bent like a question mark.

A few weeks like that and I couldn't walk without shooting pains: I had given myself sciatica. I met my first chiropractor, and my first physical therapist. I got better. I wouldn't have traded a minute. And the poet Jack Underwood's prose study of his first few years as a parent reminds me of those few weeks curled up in bed: tender, and careful, and loving, and compressed, and bent uncomfortably out of shape.

Let me explain. Before he became a parent, Underwood stalled out on a "book about uncertainty", both the Keatsian poetic kind (living in "mysteries, doubts, without any irritable reaching after fact") and the kind identified by Werner Heisenberg's uncertainty principle, a basis for quantum mechanics. Having decided to write about his small human (whose name he omits, except on the acknowledgements page), Underwood tries to connect the doubts, uncertainties and mysteries he observes around his daughter to the more quantifiable (or are they?) uncertainties of modern physics from that previous book. The result is a thoughtful and – above all – tender study of fatherhood and childhood, curled up uneasily around material from modern physics and maths.

It's a lovely volume nonetheless. New parents (if they ever find the time to read a book) will recognise themes: parents with older children will remember them. Is language really, as Wordsworth suspected, a prison, a form of violence done to infants' experience, a "dulled, violently categorical version of being alive?" Watching his baby, Underwood fears as much. As she becomes a toddler, as she acquires language, her sense of time changes: the poet can "watch you forge a temporality of your own, bruising the air with your voice, taking your first steps, upturning furniture, brandishing your future like a red plastic spoon." Her changing sense of time suggests the unmeasurable "duration" that Henri Bergson saw in human experience (like the American critic Jonathan Culler, Underwood sees the same durational presence in poems). Turning from present to future, Underwood fears for the world his daughter will see, "the long life you had been sold and told to prepare for" wrecked by adults' greed. Nonetheless he's glad "we got to be here. / and to have lived / at all."

Parenthood is, of course, political; it's also numerical (four months, five months, one year, almost two). Enjoying the "situationist, deconstructed shopping experience" of his daughter's pretend store, Underwood admits "an urge to protect you from the further story of money", from the social facts and "communal performance, through countless daily exchanges", of debt and capital. (He also, bizarrely, claims that "At the time of writing there are 1,912 five-pound notes in circulation", and 43,357 twenties: these numbers in fact – according to the Bank of England website – reflect the total *value* of all fivers and twenties circulating in 2017, in *millions of pounds*.) The closer the book gets to maths, the more it feels like an uneasy hybrid of Underwood's pre-parenthood project with the later baby-and-toddler book. Academic debates as to whether "maths is a fiction", whether numbers are ontologically real, keep up only a strained relation to a child's early months, via the false certainties demanded, and never received, in a panic attack. (Is safety real? Am I real?)

Does Underwood write primarily to his daughter (who may or may not ever read this book about her) or about his daughter to us? Sometimes I'm not sure: that uncertainty inheres in the work of parenting, so much of which can't be made clear even to other parents – they have other children, and you're working, at home, with yours. Other kinds of uncertainty come along with the work of raising a fragile child, and all children are fragile at first: "before you were born, I fought [...] against endless dark visions of dropping you." (Me too.)

But sometimes the work is play. She collects, and Underwood helps her, "your tiny sun-blanched snail shell, an acorn, two bits of string", "four old train tickets, the bright orange corner of a takeaway menu": what delights! I thought of Robert Frost's "Weep for what little things could make them glad".

"Tired of teaching you not to do things", Underwood prefers the moments when he can let his daughter be "deeply silly" instead: "we can all be chickens". Her silliness reminds him how "grateful" he is for "silliness among men", the antidote to "toxic masculine competition". Uneasy with rules that taught him how to be a guy, Underwood wonders elsewhere about robots and transhumanists and head transplantation: would he be the same guy with the same head on a new body? "What if the new [person] rejects the old knowledge in the head, refuses their name, their family, wants to start again?"

For philosophers, it's a familiar conundrum; for trans people like me, it's a trope, one among many I was surprised to find here. Underwood also admits he dislikes his speaking voice. As for his physical body, "I spend so much time inside my head that my body is like the piece of furniture the television sits on. I prefer the days when I don't have to notice it." He loves the experience of pushing a buggy: "Women find my presence benign. I feel genderless". "In your mind", he tells his daughter, "I can be a girl too [...] When I agree to be a girl you see no failure in my performance." As a child he wanted to be like St Joan: "I prefer the company of girls", he mused at age nine or ten. "I just want people to like me. My gender feels like something happening with an increasing external pressure", and puberty felt unimaginably far away.

Underwood is cisgender and straight: he says so himself. And yet his feelings about being a dad remind me of mine from back when I tried to be one, right up until I realized that I was a girl.

The poet's attempt to wrap his baby book around a prior book about physics does get awkward, but the same attempt creates unprecedented delights. A needy, delightful, vulnerable baby is, for Underwood, like a black hole: "The daughter's massive present bends the fabric" of spacetime, as of a trampoline. "It creates a curvature of spacetime", so that all things are drawn to it.

And here Underwood agrees, not just with one or two poets about the nature of parenthood, but with a main line of poems on the topic. Parenthood makes the child, at first all the time and then only sometimes, the glowing centre of a parent's universe, at once an unreadable mystery and the known centre around which all unknowns get rearranged. This child, the most important thing in the world, hence the most serious, also generates very silly surprises, juxtapositions, splurts and yoips and enthusiasms that we can only attempt to comprehend. Wordsworth's 'Immortality Ode' said so, portentously, and Thomas Hood's parody said so with rather more realism:

> Thou young domestic dove!
> (He'll have that jug off, with another shove!)
>   Dear nurseling of the hymeneal nest!
>   (Are those torn clothes his best!)
>   Little epitome of man!
> (He'll climb upon the table, that's his plan!)
> Touched with the beauteous tints of dawning life –
>   (He's got a knife!)

The great American poet Laura Kasischke took on the same contradictions more seriously in the early 2000s with her own poems about young children, among them 'Do Not Leave Baby Unattended (Manufacturer's Warning)':

> My attention
> is a net
> sewn of smoke and weight. Even

if I died, my eyes would have to be
always open underground, or blinking
in the sky. Who-

ever you are, up all night
embroidering warnings and disclaimers
on our things, sleep

easy, please.

I hope Underwood, and the rest of his family – having made it through the terrible twos – are sleeping easier tonight: I recommend his study of those years, in particular, to other parents, who have already made it through. As for the readers of poetry who might want to be parents, but are not parents yet, I'll recommend Underwood's concise and personal volume to you too, while adding as most parents would: you have no idea.

Stephanie Burt's latest book is After Callimachus *(Princeton University Press, 2020).*

ALL THE SOULS WE MIGHT HAVE BEEN

John Burnside, Learning to Sleep, *Cape, £10,*
ISBN 9781787332348
Nuzhat Bukhari, Brilliant Corners, *CB Editions, £10,*
ISBN 9781909585362

Declan Ryan on private language, risk and ambition

. . .

In 'Indelible', one of the highlights of John Burnside's latest collection *Learning to Sleep*, we encounter the generation of a private, domestic language, "our dialect of love / and common prayer, // hand-me-down terms for the heave / of a pit-shaft wall". It's a short, elegiac sequence, culminating in a portrait of the narrator's mother as she "angles her head to listen, one more song / from sixty years ago: / a falling star, a many-splendored thing / – and I see her again, caught up in a sudden fog, / the summer her youngest died". It's in a useful dialogue with two more of the book's best poems, 'Studio Weather' and 'In Memoriam'. The former is a differently-angled look at the charged vernacular of those closest to one another, "he makes up names / for everything he fears I might have missed", its language – like that described – is lived-in, trying to catch up with experience itself: "something else flickers away / from the swing of our headlamps, / a body we cannot describe / till we know it is gone". 'In Memoriam' is for Lucie Brock-Broido and has a similar urge to capture, and revisit, with a spell of words, invoking Orpheus in its poignant hopes of reunion in "one of the more elegant cafes / of Afterward".

It's in these moments that Burnside is at his best but at others a different sort of private language breaks in, a sort of souped-up poetic diction which can hobble and overload. It's sometimes found brushing shoulders with more charged, concrete writing; one poem has this lucidly animated description: "mostly, we were schooled / in absence, at our best / in languages we never hoped to learn", only to peter out into a slightly rote literariness: "story as last resort, repentance as fabric; / that linger, like a footfall in the Rock / of Ages, when we lift our eyes to see / the megafauna". Some poems are laden with this sort of thing, such as 'A Lady of the Parish', a kind of bingo-call of bad habits, "she snares you in the Book of Très Riches Heures / at Whitsun, part-exemption, part-reprieve, / a speck of gold-leaf flaking on her skin / to chalk and foil". Others drift into abstraction thanks to their urge to throw in so many shiny phrases, so much willed epiphany, the result at times a flattening of any implicit urgency, death by a surfeit of strong feeling: "in minarets of ice, // she lies down in her bed of small disdain, // her gown in shreds, / her happiness complete, // a flame in her heart / for the forfeit she paid to the hounds".

There's another thread running through here too, a slightly more mythic, folksy set of poems which largely allow Burnside the freedom to let loose but, thanks to their narrative elements, rein in too much of the untethered gallivanting. 'A Changeling' displays Burnside's skills as storyteller and scene-setter, its close-up descriptions ominous and well-judged: "my perfect / likeness in the back seat of an Austin / Cambridge, all the toffees I'd refused / preserved in a tamper-proof bag for the deposition". There's also a fine hymn to Hypnos, bringer of sleep (or not, as the case may be) blending a number of Burnside's registers, the myth-making with a fabular hauntedness to make something musical and spare: "the boys clothed all-in-green, the moonshine / flaking from their bones / forevermore, / a troupe of all the souls / we might have been". The upside of this straining for good bits does also result in some beautiful phrasing, felicitous and surprising images "the light / re-spinstering your face / by slow degrees"; "the farm cats // plucked them

from the memory of air, / so tenderly, you'd think their god had wings."
It's a risk, though, and as often it results in one too many uses of the word
"ghosting", or the adjectival equivalent of noodling around. Burnside's
verbal facility is such that even when we find him on autopilot there's
graceful phrase-making and clinching detail to be had, "women and
children / working all day / for pennies, their knuckles // ice-cold and
scabbed / with loam" but the best poems highlight how good he can be
when there's something more than a search for luminosity urging his
writing hand.

Nuzhat Bukhari's debut, *Brilliant Corners*, displays an often winning
expansiveness, managing the difficult task of casting its net wide while
also aiming for a taxonomy of words, right down to their roots. A poem
such as 'Sparkhill' feels like Bukhari at her best, mixing verbal energy with
wide reading and unguessable jumps in logic, "Outsiders say it as *Ur-du*;
clip, unsplice its delicious aspirate purr: / *Urrrthu*, a birr sound of a dove's
fanning wings as it flares for flight" – the whole poem rings with internal
music and moves fast, and far. Other poems look to unpick words
with a similar degree of attention, if without quite the same dazzle,
identifying in 'Adlestrop' (among other linguistic ghosts) a burning,
an ulcer and a wound; likewise the book's opening poem, 'Arsenal',
tunes itself to the frequency of poems about making poems, "I too,
was a maker, of forms / honed as any bullet". There are times when the
interest in words seems to become an end in itself, with mixed results – a
poem such as 'Close Relatives' opens musically but one quickly becomes
bogged down, struggling to make sense "Because a prodigal's kismet is
to / salvage infirm truths of betrayals // To coin a crippled grace, call it
poetry. / Or a love, barren of liability" while 'As Glass Frogs Catch Light',
which seems to have Hopkins lurking somewhere in its backroom, is
liable, as per one of its lines, to "drift in wobble or collapse of sound".

Bukhari tries on a wide variety of costumes, of forms, of approaches
– there's no shortage of ambition or, seemingly, of curiosity – literature,
history, science. It's a big, at times baggy, book, but there are several
high points – arresting, admirably made poems which are often good in
ways unlike one other. 'Black Icarus' has a slightly metaphysical instinct,
binding Ovid to a "stowaway / who fell out of a declining flight from
Kenya one July" – the poem allies this unnamed, doomed body with
Icarus, his father's poignant question *"surely the sky is open to us"* made

doubly resonant. It's not her only unexpected juxtaposition – as here with the falling form of a would-be escapee, in 'Tantalus' another myth becomes modernised, in this case by virtue of its name, "Tantalus morphs into a 'contact mineral'. / Silver-blue capacitor, skull-plater, salt-bomber". She also shows a talent for the prose poem, especially with 'Gross', a compellingly drawn portrayal of a model's session posing for the – unnamed – Lucian Freud, at once atmospheric and mimetically intrusive, "He stares at hip sores, an inverted nipple with hair and spot bumps around it, the other breast's skin bloated so it has a strange bluish transparency to it like an overblown balloon". The poem can't but speak to the book's other narrative of close-ups of a prone, female body, the noirish crime scene of 'Mortal Acts', "Ropey russet hair tangled in shreds of seaweed, as if on a cloth doll".

Some poems become heavy with their material. 'Self-portrait with Shark and Skull' gives Damien Hirst the prose treatment but also tries to weave in mountain climbing, mud slides, ice floes, becoming slightly choked among the expanses of its wider scale, filling its plate with enough for three or four poems. There's also a sense, across the book, of trying to touch on every pressing news story, every piquant global concern – at times forsaking the sort of closely-focused attention of the best work for an – admittedly righteous – concern to leave no atrocity or outrage out. At its worst it can lead to moments like the opening of 'Mirror Poem': "Why would I think of bodies at Auschwitz-Birkenau / spiralled like pulled roots / after making sex with you / The tenuous link is our bareness". An impossible task having been set for itself, the poem, understandably, forgivably, can't for all its Adorno-aware eloquence (it references the famous quotation) avoid sinking under its opening analogy. There's a sharpness – in both senses – to much of Bukhari's writing, unafraid and high-stakes, not least in 'Pathology', an elegy with ice, or perhaps a splash of acid, in its veins: "You twitched, spasm-jerked when I came / in but this is normal as a body transitions from compos to shut-down mode". As with the body on the slab, Bukhari presents a similarly unimpressed, scrutinising front to the other patriarchal and imperial cadavers she confronts.

Declan Ryan's latest pamphlet is Fighters/Losers *(New Walk, 2019).*

WONDER'S WILL

Wanda Coleman, Wicked Enchantment: Selected Poems, *ed. Terrance Hayes, Penguin, £9.99, ISBN 9780141995830*

Clare Pollard on genius, injustice and righteous rage

• • •

> The unread poems of true poets
> are sad. No one should love
> so hard in vain and go unnoticed.
>
> 'Obituary'

It is exhilarating to encounter a genius for the first time. But reading *Wicked Enchantment*, my exhilaration was undercut by a sickening sense of unfairness. As a scholar of literature and a poet, I should have read Wanda Coleman. In fact, this is the first UK publication of her work, and though she is now influential in the US it seems she lived in neglect and poverty for so long that people asked of her (as in the title of one poem): 'Wanda Why Aren't You Dead'? In an interview, Coleman said: "My experience has been a fairly ugly one. I know many others whose lives are also ugly, and I think writing about it is a necessity". There is no poem in this collection, brutal or beautiful, that does not leave an ugly aftertaste of injustice.

White supremacy stalks LA's streets in Coleman's horror-movie poem 'Doing Battle with the Wolf' – its pale, moonlit coat "dirty with the caked blood of my friends", it scratches on the door as children are sent to hide in the bathroom, its howl morphing into the "roar of police sirens". In 'Consciousness Raising Exercise' it is a "tornado roaming the nation uneasily / like tall blond boys in black coats with semi- / automatics". From Coleman's unhappy childhood onwards – during which she was bullied for her skin and hair – she knew her work could never be judged separately from her existence as African American, saying: "I've come to regard myself as a living, breathing statistic governed not by my individual will but by forces outside myself."

So came the "single motherhood, multiple marriages, and multiple jobs" described by Terrance Hayes in his introduction, including waitressing, filing, and editing a soft-porn magazine. A son who died of AIDS; a life of "bad money bad love scuttlebugs & cracked ceilings" ('Pseudo Dickinsonian Cento Blues'). Coleman writes with great power of what it is like to be a parent and poor:

> meatless meals of beans and corn bread/nights
> in the electronic arms of the tube
>
> mean as a bear
>
> carrying groceries home in the rain in shoes
> twice resoled and feverish with flu
>   (''Tis Morning Makes Mother a Killer')

Poverty informs not only the content of these poems but also their form. Coleman tried sci-fi as a young writer before realising that as a poor black woman in LA she was "living science fiction". In the '60s she had plays produced but found the "cost of theatre" too expensive. Poetry suits those who can only "write around the edges" of other jobs. "When you are poor, you spend a lot of time waiting," Coleman observed in an interview in *Black American Literature Forum*; she carried a notebook so as not to waste time while in line at a grocery store, or waiting for her car to be fixed. The poems have a relentless density that speaks of a poverty of space or time. The slash is a common device, more condensed than an "or" or "and", tightening her lines and creating a stomach-churning sense of a hurtling life.

It might have been different. In the 1970s, divorced, Coleman landed a writing gig on daytime soap *The Days of Our Lives*, and won an Emmy. In a 2012 self-interview for *The Nervous Breakdown*, she recounts how, eschewing TV for family and poetry, she was then offered deals by both the small, LA-based Black Sparrow Press and a record company that offered her an enormous sum for "*everything that I wrote*" (her italics). She turned the record company down, keeping her poetic integrity. Twenty years later, after her eldest son died of AIDS, she would be haunted by the thought that if "I had taken the $5 million, I would have had the funds needed to complete my college education and would have been able to better provide for my children". Several poems struggle with a mother's responsibility: "my / son called to tell me / he was beyond / the reach of my sacrifice" ('Salvation Wax').

Coleman gave up much for poetry then, and, mainly, it did not reciprocate. In her final years there were fellowships and shortlists, whilst a younger generation of poets such as Terrance Hayes told her they were fans (his *American Sonnets for my Past and Future Assassin* are directly inspired by Coleman's), but it came too late to shake that sense of being disregarded. "Imagine", Hayes says in his introduction, "how mean the famously mean Miles Davis might have been had no one taken his horn-playing seriously, and you will have a sense of Wanda's rage." Rage is a defining emotion in the poems: "in this enclosure rage is torment / torment fuels rage as I drink my own stink" ('Salvation Wax'). It is the righteous rage of unrecognised genius.

Because Coleman is a genius. She takes the sonnet form, linked to desire for the unobtainable, and remakes it for a capitalist USA of "constant strive constant drive" ('American Sonnet 24'). The object of desire is whiteness, power, victory over the other – this is a zero-sum game where "my killers always profit from my death" ('American Sonnet 66'). 'American Sonnet 85' plays with the dynamics of the traditional sonnet with dizzying originality, refiguring the sonneteer and love object as jailed and jailor: "jailer? will you still love me when I'm flit? / will you pay to hear my angst of sob and bathe in it?" The subjugator, she knows, gets off on her subjugation: "i do not know my back as well as you do / all down my crack and up it too".

'Sonnet 100', which is not included in this selection, ends with the instruction to "glory in my wonder's will" – which scholar Lizzy LeRud notes is "a Black woman's claim on a literary inheritance that's too often the purview of white men". 'Will' was Shakespeare's way of punning on his own name, whilst "wonder" is also Wanda – she has made the sonnet her own: subdued it to her "will" and positioned herself as Shakespeare's equal. Repurposing the canon allows Coleman to compete – to mock, transform, surpass. In her poems 'after' Melville, Berryman, Ginsberg, she not only takes the shapes of their poems, but uncovers the structures behind them. In 'Black Alice Laments', after Lewis Carroll, the fantasylands of English literature are exposed as a wasteland, where gold is gilt, mama a "crone":

> as i made my descent on Xanadu
> my bowels were in my throat
> my hair was gray my hands were red
> and I couldn't sing a note
> and as I warbled at the swans
> my last glass slipper broke

No escape into daydream, no permitted 'reverie' for this Alice.

Dan Chiasson calls Coleman one of the "great menders", repurposing found materials or old poems. Such a make-do-and-mend aesthetic is another way in which poverty shapes her poetics. The horror of being tested and judged repeats in scraps of administrative language. 'Aptitude Test', playing on assumptions about race, asks whether "a white couple driving thru a black neighborhood"

a)   took the wrong freeway exit
b)   are delivering turkey dinners on Thanksgiving
c)   are on their way to open up the shop
d)   are visiting their mulatto grandchild
e)   are missionaries

There is humour but also violence in the lack of possibilities, the way each question is a potential trap or trick. How "three black men standing on a corner" must be "a riot" or "a doo-wop trio". 'American Sonnet 71' is a test too: "now, let's see how you handle / a wallet. bank account. taxes. bankruptcy terrific."

In 'Salvation Wax' a mother describes how "my children eat one carefully measured cup of cornflakes three times a day". To fill such a cup is like writing a sonnet, carefully portioning out a small amount of something necessary. It is difficult to read Coleman's descriptions of struggle in these pages, however gloriously she does it. Elsewhere, in 'Letter to my Older Sister 4' she says: "it's very hard / to put one thought in front of the other". That Coleman did so with such truth and art is truly a wonder.

Clare Pollard is the editor of Modern Poetry in Translation. *Her latest book is* Fierce Bad Rabbits: The Tales Behind Children's Picture Books *(Fig Tree, 2019).*

CUPID AND PSYCHE

Anahid Nersessian, Keats's Odes: A Lover's Discourse, *University of Chicago Press, $20, ISBN 9780226762678*

Naush Sabah on polemics, intimacy and memoir

. . .

The electric pink dust jacket of *Keats's Odes* is enough to jolt one out of any sensuous reverie; while somewhat unexpected for a volume of scholarly essays it suits the boldness, clarity, and passion with which Nersessian writes. Books by academics marketed as genre-defying have been à la mode long enough to be a settled genre, characterised by fragmentary essays and musings interspersed with memoir and polemic. It's in this tradition that *Keats's Odes* is written, though it's less formally experimental than many. Nersessian borrows her subtitle directly from Roland Barthes' *A Lover's Discourse*, a rich exploration of the language of the lover in yearning – but the relation between Barthes' text and Nersessian's is elliptical and, as it's traced in the introduction, overstated.

The book admits this shouldn't be anyone's "first stop" in reading about Keats and provides a generous list of other resources including biographies, studies of Romantic poetry, and Helen Vendler's book of close readings of the odes (the most obvious point of comparison). This is all very useful to the intended general readership until we reach the final sentence of the preface and the first absurdity of the book, namely, Nersessian's conviction that "any serious appreciation of Keats's poetry begins with the section on 'Private Property and Communism' from Karl Marx's *Economic and Philosophical Manuscripts of 1844* and the first volume of *Capital*, too", a remarkable statement to make even if the book is a Marxist reading of Keats.

Keats was, of course, progressive and liberal in his politics and this makes its way into some of his poems. His early 'Sonnet on Peace' (not included in his *Poems* of 1817) very directly argues for progressive change:

> O Europe! let not sceptred tyrants see
> That thou must shelter in thy former state;
> Keep thy chains burst, and boldly say thou art free;
> Give thy kings law – leave not uncurbed the great;
> So with the horrors past thou'lt win thy happier fate!

The first poem Keats showed his friend, the Shakespeare scholar Charles Cowden Clarke, was the sonnet written for Leigh Hunt on the day Hunt was released from prison after serving two years for remarks – in his liberal journal *The Examiner* – on the Prince Regent. Keats calls this "showing truth to flatter'd state" and believes progressive values will triumph over the right-wing establishment; the lines "Who shall his fame impair / When thou art dead, and all thy wretched crew?", however, remind us that waiting for old Tories to die off isn't a strategy that's worked in the past two hundred years.

Keats's first publication was also in *The Examiner* – the sonnet 'O Solitude' – and he was firmly part of Hunt's progressive circle, taking his lead on matters of politics. The verse dedication to Hunt in the *Poems* of 1817 provides a neat summary of how Keats balances his aesthetic concerns with his politics: he spends most of the fourteen lines recalling the "glory and loveliness [that] have pass'd away" before the turn asserts that he feels as much delight and "a free / A leafy luxury, seeing I could please / With these poor offerings, a man like thee". The Tory reviewers saw this all as sufficient reason to attack Keats for his radicalism and his social class. For Nersessian, however, it is a problem that the general view of Keats's progressive politics "rests heavily on his biography and not much, if at all, on his poetry"; but if her project was to write about the political radicalism of Keats's poems, she might have chosen 'Isabella' and other poems rather than the odes which primarily explore questions around aesthetics. Such a book might have been a slimmer volume but it would have been a more convincing one, allowing Keats's radicalism to emerge from his poems and their context rather than being projected awkwardly onto them from the twenty-first century.

When she turns her incisive eye toward the facts, Nersessian writes lucid, enjoyable prose. She traces the contours of Keats's biography with the care of a lover, describing his life as if it were intimately familiar to her and the telling of it completely unrehearsed. She knows Keats from many dimensions: as the young radical, as the poet of sensuousness, a deep empath, an intense lover, and a humble orphan who left medicine for poetry and was plagued by financial uncertainty and ill health. Part of the tension inherent in Nersessian's approach to writing about Keats and the odes stems from her own sense of "unrequited love" as being someone "in possession of identities" that Keats could not have imagined or who in "a more absolute sense" doesn't matter to him or his poetry. Being someone even less imaginable to Keats, I wonder why one should care to take that particularly odd and unproductive angle in approaching close readings of the odes; it perhaps accounts for the self-consciousness in the more autobiographical sections and the more jarring political revisionism.

Nersessian is strongest when she's reading closely and writing more straightforwardly as a scholar, which she does in the essay on 'Ode to a Nightingale'. It opens with a consideration of Keats's portrait in the National Portrait Gallery as a way into writing about his tragically early death. This brief fragment of biography is aptly placed, allowing her to balance the text of the poem, the circumstance in which it was written (the anecdote from Keats's friend Brown is included), and her own insightful reading. She considers prosody ("Keats is extraordinarily careful with his caesuras: pauses within the line instead of at the end of it [...] the effect is to establish [...] a verse that moves in the undulating, slightly irregular rhythm of what Keats elsewhere calls the 'tender-taken breath' of sleep") as well as theme ("the pleasure of others is a singular affront", "expressions of the suicidal urge"), and draws out connections to Coleridge and Milton.

The essay on 'Ode to a Grecian Urn' is one of the most memorable in the book and skilfully examines the poem's depiction of dominant motifs in Greek mythology, particularly the many narratives of rape. Nersessian outlines these in a passage on Ovidian metamorphoses detailing how Greek maidens subject to rape were often transformed into something silent and nonhuman – a lake, a tree, reeds. But again, while enjoying the breadth of Nersessian's account and her ability to deftly work many sources into one narrative, I find fault in her reading and central argument: "The speaker of Keats's ode reads like a rapist. What else is that ghastly assertion, 'Beauty is truth, truth beauty'". I can't help but feel this is wilful misreading for the sake of indignant protest and reading 'anew', as scholars must, to publish. Nersessian insists 'Ode to a Grecian Urn' is about an impending rape frozen in time so it's ghastly for the speaker to equate such a scene with beauty. Yet, the ode is no more about rape than it is about animal sacrifice or playing a pipe. The lovers under the bower in the second stanza are described in terms of a chase and possible rape too, which ill fits the scene but suits her novel reading. She attempts to rescue Keats with the claim that the ode "is a critique, not a catechism: it does not want you to buy what its speaker is selling". But he's not selling what she alleges in any case: the "mad pursuit" of "maidens loth" is but one scene of many, the subject of the ode is the urn itself, its crafted silence and stillness, its permanence, the beauty of its ability to reveal truth in fictions.

Nersessian moves from this reading into discussion of university trigger warnings, classroom safety, and her own experience of being sexually harassed by a Latin teacher at an all-girls high school. It's the most clear and unambiguous section of memoir in the book and a powerful testimony: she recounts refusing to sign a statement absolving her high school despite them threatening to jeopardise her university place – a terrible abuse of power to gaslight and intimidate a female student they had failed to safeguard. Nersessian is eminently readable when writing about the personal or the technical; however, it doesn't seem to me that the sections of memoir serve the book as much more than interludes between the critical arguments and clipped insights into the writer's perspective. Every other fragment of memoir is pointedly opaque and it's clear that this is because Nersessian doesn't really want to tell us about the lover she's writing in the wake of. She must know how unsatisfactory this is for readers: if I'm going to read a lover's account, I'd like grape-bursting-on-the-palate details.

The book reads like a one-sided lover's quarrel with Keats. Nersessian is caught between awe and disappointment. She projects revolutionary intent where it isn't, such as in 'Ode to Psyche' ("he roots loudly for the obsolescence of hierarchies of all kinds [...] with the equitable side-by-sideness of Cupid and Psyche's embrace" – an impressive reach), or tries too hard to find fault and take Keats to task for writing the wrong sort of poem. 'To Autumn' is "unforgiveable" because it happens not to be about the Peterloo Massacre – Nersessian decides to block quote segments of Diane di Prima's 'Revolutionary Letter #7' through her essay as an alternative poetics to the perfect, fruitful abundance of 'To Autumn'. The more hopeful poem is one of "molotov cocktails, flamethrowers, / bombs" and with this di Prima's poem "inches past Keats" since it intimates the fall of "one unacceptable aspect of an unacceptable existence". What's unacceptable is the "human incapacity for resisting beauty", in this instance, Keats writing 'To Autumn' so soon after over a dozen protestors were killed rather than an overtly political poem like Shelley's 'The Mask of Anarchy'. Ultimately, Nersessian's jaunty prose, her erudite and attentive consideration of the odes, sags under the weight of polemic that could be said to lack negative capability.

Naush Sabah's pamphlet Litanies *is forthcoming with Guillemot Press in November. She is co-founder and editor of* Poetry Birmingham.

THE SOUND OF SIRENS

Abeer Ameer, Inhale/Exile, *Seren, £9.99,*
ISBN 9781781726105
Dom Bury, Rite of Passage, *Bloodaxe, £10.99,*
ISBN 9781780375496
Victoria Kennefick, Eat or We Both Starve, *Carcanet, £10.99,*
ISBN 9781800170704

Katrina Naomi on storytelling, passion and zest

. . .

Abeer Ameer is a wonderful storyteller. Even as she writes of torture, loss and resistance, Ameer has the lightest of touches. *Inhale/Exile* offers glimpses "between the lines of apocalypse" into ordinary Iraqis' lives under the Baathist Party's regime.

'Four Poets in a Bookshop' contains a novel's worth of characterisation and tension in one sestina. Four men meet "under the cloak / of Arabic lexicon" where the "Portrait of Saddam watches". Ameer writes not only of oppression but the means of subverting it. She is particularly astute on men's lives. In poems titled according to the subject's occupation, we meet 'The Student' who will "learn very quickly / never to give his real name" and 'The Postman' who "risked his everything" to continually fail to deliver a summons from the government, thereby saving the lives of a father and his three (remaining) sons: "Forever to be known as / Hero, Man of Honour / and World's Worst Postman". We meet the survivors, men such as 'The Diver', who dredges the Tigris, "feels the skin-to-skin connection / as he finds another body. This time with no head." The diver's family want to leave Iraq, he wants to wait for peace. "*Besides*, he says, *I can hold my breath for a   very   long   time.*"

The balance of this collection is remarkable. There is compassion at all times, even in 'Video Capture', a four-part poem about Saddam Hussein's capture and execution: "Saddam opens his mouth as they search / his hair, beard, and molars / for weapons of mass destruction." There is no revelling in his killing, even as we are reminded of "videos of the mass graves, / skulls, extracted teeth and nails / cracked bones rip hearts out."

In addition to sestinas, *Inhale/Exile* has sonnets, ghazals and freer forms, such as 'The Journey', which uses blank space to express a would-be exile's inability (or refusal) to remember:

> families walked barefoot
>
>   lost   children   on the way
> cold   they were exposed to
>   so harsh
>
> it's all God's earth
>   but she can't remember

I loved the satire in Ameer's work. In 'The Neighbour', a letter to the Baathist Party headquarters complains that a neighbour's cat has gained weight. It reads:

> *In these times of sanctions by aggressors against our most honourable state, cats should not gain weight. One can only conclude the man next door is in receipt of finances from sources external to our noble country, rebellious against The Party and Revolution.*

The cat-loving neighbour is shopped (presumed executed) because "he is known to be poor / without a regular source of income" and "an enemy of The Party and The Revolution". In the final stanza, the poet reveals the cat was, of course, pregnant.

There are bittersweet moments. An Iraqi exile takes four hours to watch a brief cookery video, in 'Learning to Make Iraqi Pickle', showing the slicing of "turnips, cauliflower and cucumber"; his Arabic is no longer fluent.

> He closes his eyes, hears the birds at sunset,
> smells baked *samoon* bread, fried aubergine.

> On his tongue, the sour sweet of cucumber,
> warm from the *bestooga* jar on the flat roof.

Inhale/Exile is a confident, humane and thought-provoking debut.

Dom Bury's first collection, *Rite of Passage*, is passionate, personal and political. It's likely to divide opinion – not because of its environmental credentials – but because of the direct nature of the work. The best of his poetry reminds me of Robin Robertson, with a Christian edge.

Bury's 'Black Bird, Nine Nails, One Child' is unusual in *Rite of Passage*, for its brevity. It's visceral, violent and very good, the bird referred to as "perfect Jesus pinned":

>   an axis
>   to swing out from,
>   little black pendulum,
>   little metronome frozen
>   mid-turn, mid-call to suffer

Disturbing. Yet another animal, a cat, is "strung up, stripped out" in Bury's 'Hunger'. The level of disturbance is heightened as the narrator intends to eat the "eight black suns" (eight embryos) in the unfortunate cat's womb.

I admired the poem 'Snow Country', in which "Lightning opens the sky // like a flung knife" and snow comes "unfurling from the sky // like a flag". Yet there are occasional clichés – "Five a.m. and I'm bolt upright" – before moments of revelation: "Grief is   the loneliest animal. It hunts   in the small hours."

Elsewhere, a reader could lose their way, such as in long poems including 'Under Dartington Redwoods' and 'What My Body Showed

Me', with little or no imagery:

> I listened
>
> so intently then I felt
> my own body leaving me   I followed it on
>
> unwilling on
> until in a clearing up ahead I could see
>
> something   waiting
> silent in the snow
>
> as if it had been there all along –
>   ('What My Body Showed Me')

In the ten-page sequence 'Metamorphosis', the intensity of the environmental concern fails to excite linguistically and I would question whether the writing transforms into poetry. Here's the fifth poem from the sequence in full:

> The alarm bells of the planet reach fever pitch –
> Covid – collective existential crisis – collapse,
> our cities no longer able to withstand foul weather,
> our nations on fire, the earth attempting to kill
> what is killing it, to avoid the canvas
> of this green miraculous earth disintegrating,
> thread by thread, thrush by thrush,
> human body by human body.

The world needs more political/environmental poetry but an ability to tell it slant can take the message further.

Eat or We Both Starve is a collection of the sensory at times so powerful it may put you off your dinner. Victoria Kennefick is hungry for experience. She explores food, sex, denial, Catholicism and bodies through taste and touch. Mouths are ever present. Meat is a danger substance, an item of desire/not desire linked to cannibalism and transubstantiation.

Kennefick opens the collection with 'Learning to Eat my Mother, where my Mother is the Teacher'. She begins with the heart: "I eat it anyway, raw, still warm. / The size of my fist, I love it." I love that Kennefick is prepared to push the reader further than they might have chosen to go. I found I went, willingly. She continues to devour. Eyes are "tougher than expected" and surprisingly "minty" (brilliant!); her mother's brain tastes "like the sound / of sirens you don't know / are screaming until they suddenly stop." Here is poetry of originality. I've read no mother/daughter poem like it. The relationship is left for us to disentangle, as we wade through the innards.

Physicality, desire and what I take to be eating disorders are potent forces in *Eat or We Both Starve*. The idea of "clean eating", cleanliness, and (self) control – spiritual and otherwise – are alluded to in "I know how cleanly I like / to punish myself" from the poem 'Alternative Medicine'. These ideas are further explored in the series 'Hunger Strikes', predominantly featuring female saints who are unable to eat (anorexia mirabilis) or who choose to eat unusual items. The fourteenth-century Catherine of Siena, for example, "vomited twigs" to avoid a suitor until she marries herself to Jesus. In the same poem, 'Hunger Strikes Catherine of Siena (1347–1380)', Kennefick writes of Catherine's relationship with "His body, others did not / understand how good it was / to kiss His holy prepuce". Indeed. In 'Hunger Strikes Angela of Foligno (1248–1309)' – and here's where you might want to put your fork down – the mystic drinks "pus from wounds of the unclean. / Christ, it is like water to me, sweet as the Eucharist". This in a bid to attain "the summit of perfection" or the ultimate closeness to God. 'Hunger Strikes Victoria Kennefick' is possibly more naked in its depiction of an eating disorder: "zip that mouth / closed like a jacket."

I admire Kennefick's writing on these themes. I'd like to see her go a little further in marrying the zest of her ideas with a daring in language. But this is a minor quibble. *Eat Or We Both Starve* is a sexy, raw and inventive first collection.

Katrina Naomi's latest collection is Wild Persistence *(Seren, 2020).*

SHADOW WORLDS

alice hiller, bird of winter, *Liverpool University Press, £9.99,*
ISBN 9781800348691
Penelope Shuttle, Lyonesse, Bloodaxe, £10.99,
ISBN 9781780375540

Stephanie Sy-Quia on excavation and illumination

. . .

Bird of winter begins with an invocation of a dog from Pompeii,
"chained hound of my underworld". Entombed beside the dog
in its glass case is the form of a "burnt child / found curled on vesuvius's
shoreline",

> whose hunched body carries me back
> to the linen sheets and lace counterpane
>
> in my mother's house where the garden
> hides dark sheds hung with limp pheasants
>
> where rhododendrons flash
> slippery purple pleasures

> where the dead eye of the bird bath
> looks up   but sees nothing

Linen sheets, lace counterpane, bird bath, shed hung with game, and the stark obscenity of rhododendrons: these are all the markers of a self-immuring gentility, violent beneath its veneer. This is the counterpane as fig leaf, as counterfeit prurience, as the bourgeois prudishness which presumes to position itself as the only thing which can "protect the children" and then does not. In summoning Pompeii, hiller has made this childhood home into an interred zone of Derridean inflections: it is both origin and ruin; the origin which has suffered the ruin and been made riddlic by it.

But hiller does not suffer the riddle. This is a book about the sexual abuse and grooming hiller suffered as a child, something which she makes explicit in a closing note: "To excavate my own history of being groomed, and then sexually abused as a child, and along with the adolescent aftermath, was not easy", she writes in 'Living beyond sexual abuse'. "Writing these poems, the shadow worlds of Pompeii and Herculaneum were a source of intense illumination for me." (The note includes a list of numbers for organisations working to help survivors of (child) sexual abuse.) Trauma, like the forms of those killed by Vesuvius, is that which is snowed over, interred under metres of ash and pumice and earth. It is the event which bifurcates the body between unbidden underworld and surface form; it is the barrow visible in the tissue memory of the land and it is the slow accretion of stifling particles over time. To heal, it must be exhumed, catalogued; plaster casts made from its voids.

Mining her own teenage medical notes, captions from the sites of Pompeii and Herculaneum, and deriving erasure and concrete poems from various sources, hiller offers extraordinary resilience and moments of immense, liberatory tenderness. Her poems are neither explicit nor euphemistic: part of the work being carried out here is a denunciation of poetry's sometime trade in euphemism. Instead, the camera moves to those who are partial or silent witnesses to the crime: doctors, the bird bath. In 'december 1976', our speaker informs us:

I want to sleep curled
In the bottom of the freezer
Where the lost petit pois lie
Like bullets among
The plucked pheasants

Pheasants again! And there is the echo, in "where the lost petit pois lie" of "full fathom five" and with it, the sense of estrangement from the sunlit zone. In the palindromic 'becoming your channel of pearl', the lines rise and descend again, a foray into sexuality hampered by trauma loop. In 'love me', a poem that flickers achingly between childhood memory and adult present, an egg is cracked: "open two jagged cups // slip the yolk / from lip to lip without / piercing its round". As hiller writes on her blog, "Healing comes through cleaning up the damage, and then moving beyond it, to clearer waters and moments of love and joy, which more truthfully define us and let us know who we are. I wanted *bird of winter* to honour these good elements, which enabled me to resist, and ultimately reclaim myself." This is a harrowing book, yes, but ultimately, with its invitation to "billow forth the wrecks we hold", with its emphasis on resistance and joy, it is a staggeringly beautiful piece of life-affirming work.

Penelope Shuttle's *Lyonesse* takes a similar impetus for a different project. Lyonesse is the land to the south-west of Land's End in Cornwall, submerged by the sea over the course of a single night at the end of the eleventh century, and of which only St Michael's Mount and the Scilly Isles remain. Like Pompeii and Herculaneum, it is also a buried place, one which Shuttle uses to explore both her grief for her late husband (the poet Peter Redgrove) and climate change. "[Lyonesse] is real, had historical existence", she writes in her preface. "It is also an imaginary region for exploring depths. It holds grief for many kinds of loss." The emphasis on a plurality of loss is apposite, for this collection is a double bill: the second part, 'New Lamps for Old', more explicitly deals with her negotiation of her personal grief, and learning to live in its aftermath.

In the first part of the collection, 'Lyonesse', Shuttle takes a potent site of the British mythical imaginary (Lyonesse is charged with Arthurian associations, and acts as our very own Atlantis) and gives it playful treatment. There are rambunctious poems featuring lions as a pun off the placename ("They like mauling   treasure chests / licking shrimp off dead men's vests"). They stride the sand and streets of Lyonesse, which, in its antediluvian form, contained "gownshops" which "took satin for granted, silk / was cheaper than salt" (then the swallowing storm comes: "Glimmery Bourse and crystalline Parliament, drowned. Even the rococo-style abattoirs. Gone.") 'The Foster Brothers of Kernow Speak' features the usurpation of a Cornish accent ("Running into us ole boyos", "eh bro?"), and this critic is unsure as to what end. Sadly, many of these poems feel as if they fall short of an otherwise rich overarching premise.

Lyonesse's most successful poems are the ones that address their emotions head-on, without the duck-and-dodge of humour. In 'My Friend', we are given a glimpse into the submerged, lost parts of a life:

Sometimes I glimpse my friend
glinting beneath
the shape-shift silvers
of the waves
I don't know how she got down there
so near and so far from the blessed isles nor how long she'll stay
but there she is
        fathoms deep
pacing the boulevards of Lyonesse
searching each casement and porch
of water-wounded temple and storm-shattered fane
hauling her sorrow through the coral crossways
She isn't alone   my friend
Others while away the long hours
treading alley and ope of that green translucency
looking for the ones   who will never be found
down there in a city laid-out   in its own legend

Glimmering in the weft of this poem is also an excoriation of hubristic human civilisation (the belief in one's own legend): this is a compassionate, complex levelling of two emotional scales (the friend and the lost world, the personal and the mythic). In 'glance', however, which comes after the shift to 'New Lamps for Old', there is an Orpheus-like encounter with the departed which manages immense emotional heft with a lightness of imagery:

> I glance over my shoulder
> There you are
> No I haven't forgotten you
> But my life's
> Had other things to do
> Years and days lost at sea
> The silver salty snappy sea

Elsewhere in 'New Lamps for Old', in the long poems 'Swarthmoor Hall, Ulverston', 'Under Ragged Stone Hill' and 'break of day / this one evening', the cycles of the natural world are seen taking their course, modelling life after loss. This works for personal grief, but feels placatory in the face of climate change. The overlapping of climate grief (or issuing of climate caution) with personal grief is a delicate endeavour and not, I think, wholly successful: we are all destined to survive the loss of loved ones, but the world can still be saved, even if only partially. It is the fatalism of a certain type of climate grief to which I am opposed: it is incumbent on all of us to rouse the necessary will and mettle for hope, and action. The warning is issued via *Lyonesse*, but nothing much more is done with it: must we wait for the waves to come for us, just as inevitably as we will have to live after the deaths of those we love? I hope not.

Stephanie Sy-Quia's debut collection Amnion *will be published by Granta in November.*

THE LANDSCAPE WITHIN ME

Jason Allen-Paisant, Thinking with Trees, *Carcanet, £10.99,*
ISBN 9781800171138
Ralf Webb, Rotten Days in Late Summer, *Penguin, £9.99,*
ISBN 9780141992730

Mantra Mukim on listening, working and naming

· · ·

Jason Allen-Paisant's *Listening with Trees* brings to forest trees a new "way of listening". Listening through layers both opaque and permeable, he registers the historical absence of Black people from pastoral. Walking the English woodlands, his speaker, stopping to listen to the rhododendrons, seagulls and oaks in autumn, finds this soundscape filtered through a history of forced labour, encompassing the plantation economy in Jamaica – for him, a leisurely walk appears a rare privilege. While these poems attempt to renew the pastoral lyric with their attention to the landscape and to community, they also update the genre's traditional playlist. Alongside the usual birdcalls and pulsations of spring one hears the noise of injustice – those very conditions that once made pastoral (both the poetic mode and the ability to access nature as nature) the refuge of a fortunate few, and still keep it out of reach for others.

Listening, in this case, means surrendering to the authority of a biome: the already over-mapped and taxonomically exhausted English landscape. 'Naming' (the title of the poem) is a mode of caring engagement, but can also become a means of possession:

> because
> a name is
>   reassurance a comfort in the flesh
> to hold
>
> these songs in the trees
> so something could be mine

Names are only "nearly right", missing their mark and undercut by what will always remain nameless. For this poet naming does not by itself blunt experience, unlike for Rilke who considered naming responsible for "murdering all my things"; what makes Allen-Paisant uncomfortable is the impossibility of naming again, of being excluded from the inaugural scene of naming, Adam and Linnaeus being white men: "The urge I feel is / to give things names but // everything is already / named". The poem goes on to state:

> All I can handle
> is nature under fingernails
> my grandmother planting
> negro yams
> shaping the land
>
> All I can handle is the landscape within me
> not scenery
> spread out on a canvas

This "landscape within" interrupts and spills over the landscape outside, setting up an incessant dialogue between the pastoral woodlands and a past life that was "un- / pastoral / The woodland was there / not for living in   going for walks / or thinking". The mid-line pause, perhaps denoting the schism between the two lives, does not take anything away from the gift of thinking, something the collection cherishes; it allows the speaker to register sounds whose lineage lies not within the landscape but with the human voice that describes it. Those daffodils commemorated by Wordsworth, and a staple of postcolonial curricula worldwide, need updating: "It's time to write about daffodils / again to hear // a different sound / from the word // daffodil". To hear this new sound, one is invited to cross the threshold into something "accidental / so entire so free", away from an exclusive lyric past and beyond the inherited traumas of slave labour. This crossing, the speaker of poems like 'Black Walking' informs us, is not only a physical passage but a leap over the precipice of racial asymmetry. "[T]his is a land you can take your time with // these peaks are safe   I won't need to run", says the speaker.

Some of this collection's most memorable poems are about dog walking, which turns the rest and renewal promised by the landscape on its head, as the speaker is "troubled by this normalcy // in which the dog / gets everything it wants". This "normalcy", portrayed as the apotheosis of pastoral idleness, continues to discomfort. Here from 'Essay on Dog Walking (II)' is a litany of affections: "The pampering / the caressing / the spoiling / the doting / the fussing /   over the dog", followed by the rot that is "hidden from view" and "reminds him / his ancestors / were property /   less than these animals".

In *Rotten Days in Late Summer*, this rot is the very architecture of our lives. Ralf Webb's speaker puts his ears to trees, to machines and to his lover's body to listen to another kind of hum – one that heralds the end of things. Webb has a gift for brisk opening lines – "I can see them, all my tools laid out"; "Copper Stench, low-frequency fly-drone"; "Don't worry. I'm not turning religious"; "Your mouth is different from how I / remember it"; "Your new wingtips are having difficulties". This has the effect of dropping us at once into scenes where 'thinking' or resting is scarcely possible either for the speaker or the reader, nor is such rest desired. Interpersonal relations and aspects of industrial work are made carefully indistinguishable: but there is also another kind of work – the work of listening, of letting sounds, affects, even "metal fillings", take over one's "physical intelligence". Except that the work of listening in these poems involves listening to the actual sounds of work – the industrial shifts, cleaning of toilets, hoovering of floors.

Some of Webb's poems lead you by the hand through the West Country, directing your gaze as in 'White Ennox Lane': "Take the road by the cluttered graveyard. / Here, the dead stay dead. / But the headstone moss is like stubble". In others, the speaker is less sure, if not of their surroundings then of what those surroundings mean. This uncertainty is what makes Webb's collection, especially the love poems sprinkled through it, a work of generosity. By not defining his experience, or claiming authority over it, Webb's speaker privileges over himself those that he befriends, works alongside, makes love to and mourns.

It is in loving that we commit most intensely to the work of listening, allowing ourselves to be guided by a voice not ours: for this reason, Webb swaps out the first person for an ineluctable "you". "Abstract processes" and "hard work", which house both the self-enclosed world of love and the rot that threatens it, provide optic and sonic contexts for 'Love Story: Rotten Days':

> I can see them, all my tools laid out
> On the counter, hands hovering
> Above them, trying to glean
> The future of each. You understood
> Their immediate functions, and moreover
> Understood their functions in the final,
> Abstract processes. The beginning
> Of the night-shift: let loose
> Our fantastic pissing contest.
> A complete surrender to overheads,
> All of your blemishes lightened,
> And grease in the corners of your mouth,
> Your stalled moustache. The moths
> And may bugs, ending themselves.

The mass suicide of summer bugs, perfunctory and quick, could perhaps be a slightly cynical corollary for the lovers described in the collection, but it also captures the pathos of seasonal transience. Webb's poems are not interested in exchanging physically demanding industrial work, its exhaustions and precarities, for an idealised pastoral ripe with love and intimacy. The physical language and rhythms of work, gruelling as they might be, court those of affection and care. Coming to terms with his father's illness, the speaker of 'Diagnostics' deploys a mixed register: "Days hover around his eyes, scavengers, / and pour into them. Then back out again. / Marrow is drained, replaced, like engine oil."

Speaking is forbidden in this landscape. The human voice is subdued either by "archaic wrench" or "weeping oils", or overcome by the mouth's desire to consume. The lovers' mouths in 'Love Story: Boys at the Age of Twenty' have to pause to be able to love: "We left, to stop our mouths with the sea. / And started talking only in quotes". Counterpoised to these affectionate silences is the brutality of 'You Can't Trust Violence', where one speaker is so disgusted by another's difference as to want to force their silence:

> What would it feel like:
> a metal pipe, slapped into an open palm,
> then elevated, then struck down,
> into the mouth of that queer.
> Dear Dad, Sir, it would be so pretty,
> the wincing crunching jewellery.
> God's hand closes and makes a fist.
> The paths folds in on itself. Keys, ignition.
> Daniel thinks that justice is a feeling,
> potted and tended by fathers,
> and passed down along a line.

In these quick-paced but tender poems, Webb tracks the beauty and rot of pastoral. His final sequence emerges from the factory, with a "nix to the global crises, the endless ecological traumas", and search for succour among trees. "The tree-brains are shedding their pollen. / I am shedding all pretences, refining / My attentions." Yet there remain signs – literally – of how relentlessly the present is vanishing: "The red signs in the ancient woodland, near the ruins, say TREE CUTTING."

Mantra Mukim is currently a doctoral candidate in the English department at University of Warwick.

A WIND TOO STRONG TO BREATHE

Fred D'Aguiar, Letters to America, *Carcanet, £10.99,*
ISBN 9781800170087
Yousif M. Qasmiyeh, Writing the Camp, *Broken Sleep, £10.99,*
ISBN 9781913642358

James Byrne on re-memory, return and transcending time

. . .

L*etters to America*, Fred D'Aguiar's new collection from Carcanet (his ninth published in the UK), returns me to Toni Morrison, specifically her idea of "re-memory" first posited in *Beloved* (1987) in relation to the denied experiences of slaves. Re-memory is the attempt at physically or mentally recovering the historical that has never been recorded or fully acknowledged. An attempt to remember memories. In reading D'Aguiar's oeuvre, the concept appears to weave through his work, from an early novel, *The Longest Memory* (1995), which documents the story of a young slave trying to escape a Virginian plantation in 1810, to a genre-bending autobiography about surviving those deadly Cs (Covid and cancer) titled *Year of Plagues*, to be released later this year. In *Letters*, D'Aguiar re-remembers events from a childhood in Guyana, but also more recent history including LA protests against Trump and the tragic shooting at Virginia Tech (where he taught before being appointed

Professor of English at UCLA). For D'Aguiar, as for Morrison (and Yousif M. Qasmiyeh, who I will come to later), going back is a kind of perpetual return, a painful refusal to concede against the weight of violence.

Letters to America opens with a series of fairly brisk, delicate lyrics which look across time and space. These are highly atmospheric poems that work busily like short film collages. 'Atlantic Ground' eerily traces itself within the violence of the slave route, where "bones assemble / Pulled together by coral music anchors". Psychogeography and psychohistory collide frequently throughout these *Letters*, but D'Aguiar's ambition extends to a third term, what I would call psychoanima, where space is explored through the animal:

Dark finds me waiting for a world
Birds bring to my patch of green,
Wings sow light, songs keep time.

('Downtown L.A.')

blue jays pick up with articulate claws, fly four floors and drop,
but lucky nine lives rabbit lands, thuds, looks hurt,

stays still for seconds, as if lost in dream space,
staggers away, and another jay grabs it, until we intervene

('Black Lives Matter')

The final "we" reminds me of a comment D'Aguiar made in the Q&A of a lockdown reading last year: his aesthetic is increasingly concerned with how "oneness becomes a we-ness". In 'Black Lives Matter', the jays of the poem hunt down a rabbit until the communal pronoun offers protective action. The animal is eventually saved, for the time being at least, wrapped in a t-shirt as the predatory jays are chased away, tipping their "wings for another zone", which suggests the violence continuing elsewhere.

The gesture of community and communal response is key to D'Aguiar's *Letters*, not least in his defining title poem, an abecedary which takes place during a protest march in LA, but also moves through the author's childhood in Guyana and life as a young man in London. It's a dizzying, playful sweep through the alphabet which requires multiple readings and a loosening of the collar. Not waiting to ask if we're sitting comfortably, the poem simply takes off, opening in the middle of a conversation:

'Ah neva seen this before in all ma years'.
Testify, Sis. How we grew accustomed,
Spoiled almost, by decorum, now try
Mosquito larvae cultivating at speed
In standing bodies of water. Pigeons
Flock rooftops, twist, launch, shout
As one, spin sky, turn skulls porous.

Car repair shop drills sing industry.
Tires feel out parking, meters freed.
First horn blare triggers this chorus.
Step up pistons, fire motor mouths,
Say our only worry is our worst fears
Come true. Mosquito straw proboscis
Drinks from my arm, bam! Adios asterisk.

·

But, really, am I eyeballing an armoured truck?
('Letters to America')

Note how the poem's rhythm snaps back elastically, in disbelief, as the national guard arrive at the scene. 'Letters to America' moves at speed but its consistent thread is the threat of power. Published after, but written just before the killing of George Floyd, D'Aguiar documents those who sleep with "one eye open // Breath held when police cruise by", (re-)remembering how it was "too late / For Troy, for Trayvon". D'Aguiar honours the dead, but measures this against the ineptitude of government policy. As he writes with painful irony: "Black lives matter but blue lives matter more."

Because it is written across but, ultimately, transcends time, it would be too easy to deem *Letters to America* an epochal poetics. There's a willed persistence to speak against injustices from colonialism to capitalism as well as to warn against the future, politically, but also ecologically. 'Burning Paradise', one of the strongest poems in the book, recounts the tragic 2017 Camp wildfire in California, where we find a sky "skinned red" and a "wind too strong to breathe". In the forest, as with earlier poems in *Letters*, there's the suggestion of a darkness being unnavigable, "so thick / we can't cut through". Again, despite the threat of oblivion, the communal "we-ness" within the space of re-memory reveals D'Aguiar's concerns for the planet mirroring those he expresses for social unrest and injustice. What is revealed ultimately, in the final (insistently overlong) poem 'Calypso', which takes aim at big tech companies and sees Brexiteers as "frogmarched by idealogues", is a poetics "built on love, and love is all I can trust".

I've long admired D'Aguiar's poetry for its musicality, which rarely has anything less than perfect pitch, even when taking on extended narrative or dramatic monologue (the 'King David' poem about a self-styled Rasta chef in Jamaica is a good example of this). Still, there's a shift in these *Letters*, even more swing and dare in the language and an unflinching political activism. Put simply, D'Aguiar is writing the most accomplished and interesting work of his life.

Yousif M. Qasmiyeh's *Writing the Camp* is a debut of remarkable enquiry into the idea of the refugee camp, specifically the Baddawi camp in Lebanon where Qasmiyeh was once based with his family. With its exploration of lyric address, fragmented sequential passages and stretches of parablesque meditational prose, Qasmiyeh is comfortable writing through (but also resisting) various poetic forms. Adept as philosopher or poet, frequently amalgamating both, the texts here are tonally confident yet vulnerable. This is an open poetics, personal and speculative, confessional yet innovative. There's a waft of Derrida in the more conceptual moments in considering Qasmiyeh's central question: what is a refugee camp? The poet weaves in archival considerations in providing the impossible answer:

> Only refugees can forever write the archive.
> The camp owns the archive, not God.
> For the archive not to fall apart, it weds the camp
> unceremoniously.

The question of a camp archive is also the question of the
camp's survival beyond speech.
('Refugees are dialectical beings')

As in D'Aguiar's *Letters*, the threat of violence looms throughout
Qasmiyeh's poetics. Even language itself predicts danger, the dialectical
"a spear of noises" to the refugee (who is also a collision of dialects, as
the camp more broadly is). As a place of intense precarity, death is never
far away in the refugee camp. Even to reach Baddawi camp you have to
pass the cemetery, writes Qasmiyeh. Death is both seen and unseen,
sometimes capitalised like God, both characters prowling through the
collection. The writing is both disturbing and captivating and, where
it chooses to be, furnished with poetic flourishes that transform what
is observed into what is revealed:

The moon is the birthmark of the refugee.

His birth equates to the mauling of his entire body.
('A sudden utterance of the stranger')

We walk, so we think, never in the absolute presence of one
another, breathing the blindman's stick.
('A soliloquy before time')

Writing the Camp branches out the poet's family tree; relatives who
stayed in the camp ("My mad grandfather who remained behind as
dead") and others who survived, made it out. Several sections observe
a mother figure and are so intimate they read like love poems. In one
such section, it is possible for language and hope to live together, in the
unwritten. The mother tries to write her name for the very first time to
inscribe her son's new notebook. She succeeds, but Qasmiyeh knows he
will have to fill up the remaining pages alone. Ultimately he leaves the
camp, documenting the process of claiming asylum with compassion
for the other, yet hinting subtly at the trauma endured.

She did to me what a friend would normally do for a friend or a
lover for another lover – she held my hand very tightly [...] I feel

the need to go back to that terminal and ask her what it meant to touch a stranger.

Having survived the brutality of the camp, Qasmiyeh (now at Oxford University as a postgraduate) asks how can we work through the past and move towards a future. For Qasmiyeh, the past works through the body. And it is through the body and in darkness where memory, he tells us, "looks down at its feet", which suggests going back to something walked through. Qasmiyeh re-remembers, ultimately to reawaken time denied, where the past is pulse "as the future". This is perhaps a positive note of survival. However, in this idea of "pulse" lives the trauma of memory and the loss of time, suggesting a negotiation which is vital and ongoing. *Writing the Camp* is epic in scope and I will, no doubt, re-read it for years to come. It heralds a major new voice in British poetry.

James Byrne's next collection is Places You Leave, *forthcoming from Arc. He co-edited* I am a Rohingya: Poetry from the Camps and Beyond *(Arc, 2019).*

A GARMENT FOR THE FLAGSTONES

Joyelle McSweeney, Toxicon & Arachne, *Corsair, £10.99,*
ISBN 9781472156051

Lucy Mercer on wormholes, bacteria and toxic poems

. . .

Welcome to hell – you will be dragged into it, you are already in it. Joyelle McSweeney's *Toxicon & Arachne* explodes out from and traverses across this catastrophic, militarised, toxic, surreal, plastic, bony realm that foams into everywhere. Unstatic, nonlinear, spooling across exorbitantly large macrocosmic and microscopic material-bacterial-conscious scales, *Toxicon & Arachne* shows what it is possible to do in poetry that is simply not possible elsewhere. The words uncanny or extraordinary seem the wrong descriptive choices here – it is a frothing "boanmeal" spectacular, it is terrifying. I can't really convey what it felt like to me, falling into and through its wormholes, except that when I looked up "metacarpals" I found out finger bones extend far deeper into the hand than I thought. Suddenly, what I thought was shielded by a protective layer was in fact squishier, more fragile, horrifying and stranger than I thought. I stared at my own hand unsettled, unable to unsee this new fact. An inability to unsee is perhaps one way of thinking about the trajectory of the poetic vision of this book, barraged as it is by its unchosen encounters.

A double volume in two parts, *Toxicon & Arachne* is like a Möbius strip with two twists or sides that darkly mirror each other unequally, push-and-pull. *Toxicon* opens with 'Detonator', which serves as an epigraph or hole to fall into and is followed by 'Ars Poetica', an overview of sorts of McSweeney's radical vision of a (necro)poetics – of which more shortly. *Toxicon* is devoted among other things to the tuberculosis bacterium that killed Keats and toxic gestation, drilling deep down inside as well as outwards. Prefaced by 'Terminator', the second part, *Arachne*, is a set of (at times) more direct meditations adjacent to and encircling the death of the poet's third daughter in early infancy. McSweeney has spoken of how, after Arachne's death, the preoccupations in *Toxicon* became prophetic to her – and this grim suture, where the future lies in the past, turns the strip back onto itself.

It is difficult to descend into *Toxicon* without the right accessories or amulets – such as handgrenades, pomegranate seeds – in this case, McSweeney's concept of the Necropastoral, which is intrinsic to the book and is conceptually scaffolded in her monograph *The Necropastoral: Poetry, Media, Occults* (University of Michigan Press, 2014). To briefly summarise using some of McSweeney's terms, the Necropastoral is a non-rational, political-aesthetic Hadean zone focused on non-human material processes such as viruses, toxins, weeds. This realm is a deathly, obscene, nonlinear site that irrupts and continually re-emerges in our collapsed ecological time in the Anthropocene, where the past continually collides with the present. A shadow other to Keatsian poetic-lyric ideals of aesthetic beauty as a static, pristine, fenced-off Arcadia, the Necropastoral has its own aesthetics: corroded, corrupt, stinking, decayed, obscure, poisonous, wounded, forever-interconnected, the seeping of beings and bodies noisily back out of the earth. In this the Necropastoral is also apocalyptic, redemptive – not in terms of being restorative, but that things literally can't be wasted or forgotten – they never leave, but circulate, violently, always re-resurrecting in spectacular and exhibitionist ways. Many poems in *Toxicon & Arachne* refer to murder victims, snuff sites, painful deaths, war, trenches. McSweeney's gathering and stitching together of so many skeletal fragments also reminds me of writer and Jungian psychoanalyst Clarissa Pinkola Estés' mythical archetype of *La Loba*, a wolf woman who collects bones in the desert and sings skeletons alive again.

Toxicon also presents a crown of toxic sonnets for Keats; I think the name of the bacterium, broken down – *My-co-bacterium tuberculosis* – seems apt in relation to thinking about these poems that are guided by a bacterial point of view, that connect the poet to the character of Keats, and later connect Keats's lungs to the lungs of Arachne who could not breathe. Co-writing: writing as a form of material process, a kind of ecosemiotics where bacteria and viruses direct the hand as much as thoughts, enter thought, leave poisonous trails. Flesh, text, toxic, biomaterial worlds commingle in a form of cultural ecology. Described by McSweeney as a "quiver of poisoned arrows" (toxin and arrow sharing an etymological root), the collection's vision of lyric violence that permeates, invades, sinking unchecked through tissue and paper alike, brings to mind Andrea Brady's meditations on "drone poetics" – and the impact of the hypervisibility of drones on the contemporary lyric (drones too, feature in *Toxicon*).

Veering through sonnets, sestinas, free verse in a "sound-infused hyperdiction", *Toxicon & Arachne* also manifests stylistically an intense resistance to adhering to any definitive poetic mode, which I read as a resistance to what Aditi Machado has outlined in her excellent essay *The End* (Ugly Duckling Presse, 2020) as "the conceptual moneys of poetry", which depend on strategies not to overwhelm "the Reader" in order to generate consumable poetic value. Machado's list of these don't-do conventions could all be applied to *Toxicon & Arachne*: "sonic excess", "multilingualism", "arcane references", "word play, especially punning", "emotion", "abstraction", "big words". The book's multivalenced, long poems, as well as frequent use of money metaphors, engage in this fight against received notions of value, of digestibility. Rather: vomit, spew, scream, be dragged along. It is tempting to say that McSweeney's poems in this sense have a kind of maximalist aesthetics of excess, but rather I think they are poems of maximum precision, a kind of poetic empiricism. To cut extracts out and quote them in a review – this act feels like a disservice to the book's project and to the structure of the poems, which lengthily move as an open text.

Too, *Toxicon & Arachne* as maternal writing presents a violent, messy materiality where inner is outer and outer is inner. The garments, pockets and gloves recurring throughout remind me of Ursula K.

Le Guin's 'The Carrier Bag Theory of Fiction' (1986), which redefines technology as a cultural carrier bag, a container, a womb, as found in 'Ars Poetica': "pulled from the Seine with a seine net. With a purse seine", or

> The puddled cloth, the placket of blood
> like a garment for the flagstones
> below the smashed skull
> sewn on the bias
> the seam lies flat

No one is exempt from being gathered in, gathering or imbricated in these Pandora's boxes, careering through the wreckage coated in lotions, potions, full of medications, gems, "bedazzled" – there is no relief from the endless chemical spills, extraction, exploitation in this "*ceaseless report*" patterned together by sound, where nothing can fly forward except a toxified poetic logic.

Likewise, the book's engagement with a communal history of birth and death feels synonymous with, though by no means exclusive to, motherhood – to have a child is also always to bring a death into the world, to excavate a grave in the future. The poems in *Arachne* inhabit this "endzone" in an unsentimental mode that is acute, unbearable, a personal testimony that I feel unable to comment on. Like a toxic arrow, death has a twin movement of rising out of the sky (and keeping rising) – and dropping into the bottom-most floor of the basement (and keeping crashing down). The final poem in *Arachne*, and the book, ends with this impossible dual movement, impossibly possible in poems:

> I summon all mine vanity
> virility and fertility
> and crash my plane
> into the abandoned nursery
>
> & break my brainstorm down
> I mean my brainstem
> starved of oxygen
> eating itself
> emitting its bleat

like a nameless weed
on the edge of the galaxy
fringing the galaxy's cunt
in that wrecked room
cool nursery
the popsong plays
in eternity
on the toy turntable
and a curtain lifts
impossibly
as the vinyl record spins
it feels the morning sun
on its original face
('Morning Wants an Eidolon...')

Lucy Mercer's first collection, Emblem, *is forthcoming in 2022 from Prototype.*

CONTRIBUTORS

'Gbenga Adeoba is the author of *Exodus* (University of Nebraska Press, 2020) and *Here is Water* (APBF/Akashic Books, 2019) • Rachael Allen's first collection of poems, *Kingdomland*, is published by Faber • Natalya Anderson won the 2017 Moth Poetry Prize for her poem 'A Gun in the House', and the 2014 Bridport Prize for her poem 'Clear Recent History' • Polly Atkin is the author of *Basic Nest Architecture* (Seren, 2017), *Much With Body* (Seren, 2021), and *Recovering Dorothy: The Hidden Life of Dorothy Wordsworth* (Saraband, 2021) • Sheri Benning's fourth collection of poetry is *Field Requiem* (Carcanet, 2021) • Colin Channer's books include the novella *The Girl With the Golden Shoes* and the poetry collection *Providential* • Edward Doegar is a poet and editor living in London • Ian Duhig's *New and Selected Poems* is due from Picador in December and is a Poetry Book Society Special Commendation • Sarala Estruch's debut pamphlet, *Say*, will be published by flipped eye in October • Owen Good is the translator of Krisztina Tóth's short story cycle *Pixel* (Seagull, 2019), and a winner of the Asymptote Prize for his translations of Tóth's poetry • Mina Gorji is Associate Professor at the University of Cambridge. Her debut collection is *art of escape* (Carcanet, 2020) • Philip Gross is a prize-winning poet, for adults and young people, who thrives on collaborations, with writers and across the arts • Sylvia Legris' new poetry collection, *Garden Physic*, is forthcoming with New Directions in November and Granta in 2022 • Tim Liardet has been shortlisted for the T.S. Eliot Prize twice, and has produced ten collections of poetry • Kathryn Maris's third collection is *The House with Only an Attic and a Basement* (Penguin, 2018) • Nyla Matuk is the author of *Sumptuary Laws* and *Stranger* and editor of an anthology, *Resisting Canada* • Shane McCrae's most recent books are *Sometimes I Never Suffered* and *The Gilded Auction Block*, both published by Corsair • Momtaza Mehri is a poet and essayist. She is a co-winner of the 2018 Brunel International African Poetry Prize • Melissanthi (1907–1990) was a Greek poet, teacher and journalist • Brian Robert Moore is a literary translator originally from New York City, whose translations include *Meeting in Positano* by Goliarda Sapienza (Other Press) and *A Silence Shared* by Lalla Romano (forthcoming, Pushkin Press) • K Patrick is a writer based in Glasgow. They have been shortlisted for the White Review Poets' Prize, the White Review Short Story Prize and the Ivan Juritz Prize • Yvonne Reddick is a poet and researcher. She is the recipient of a Leadership Fellowship from AHRC, for research on poetry of the Anthropocene • Amy Roa is a poet from Brooklyn, New York • Goliarda Sapienza (1924–1996) began writing poetry in the 1950s while she was working in the film industry in Rome • Karen Simecek is an Associate Professor in Philosophy at the University of Warwick • Taylor Strickland is a poet and translator from the US • Krisztina Tóth has published eight volumes of poetry, six of short stories, and one novel in her native Hungarian • Karen McCarthy Woolf was awarded a Fulbright scholarship to join the Promise Institute of Human Rights at UCLA as a poet in residence exploring law, poetries and ecologies of space.

13 October 2021
7pm BST on Zoom

The Poetry Review autumn issue launch on Zoom

Readers: **Rachael Allen**, **Sheri Benning**, **Sarala Estruch** and **Shane McCrae**. The event will be introduced by *Review* Editor **Emily Berry**.

Tickets are free but space is limited. Please book online at bit.ly/reviewaut21launch

Image by Kate Dehler. katedehler.com

THEPOETRYSOCIETY

THE

Poetry Review

Podcast

The best poetry conversation...

Subscribe to *The Poetry Review* **podcast series** for illuminating conversation, diverse views and resonant readings – with poets including Denise Riley, Raymond Antrobus, Don Paterson, Fiona Benson, Ishion Hutchinson, Chelsey Minnis and – just added – Selima Hill, Rachel Long, Luke Kennard and Mary Ruefle

Free download • Find us on Soundcloud & Spotify • Subscribe via iTunes

Selima Hill (photo: Jill Furmanovsky); Rachel Long (photo Amaal Said); Luke Kennard

poetry 10nd0n

NATIONAL POETRY LIBRARY PRESENTS
POETRY LONDON'S 100th ISSUE

JOIN US FOR A STELLAR LINE-UP OF POETS
INCLUDING CHRISTOPHER REID, MONIZA ALVI,
FRED D'AGUIAR, DAN O'BRIEN
& ROMALYN ANTE

Plus MALIKA BOOKER presenting the winners of the
2021 Poetry Prize

Hosted by ANDRÉ NAFFIS-SAHELY

SATURDAY 23 OCTOBER, 7–8.30PM
SOUTHBANK CENTRE, ROYAL FESTIVAL HALL,
LEVEL 5 FUNCTION ROOM
TICKETS £7 via southbankcentre.co.uk

~

POETRY LONDON'S 100th ISSUE:
CELEBRATING 33 YEARS OF ONE OF THE UK'S
GREATEST POETRY MAGAZINES

Unique block-printed hardcover bumper edition featuring
100 pages of exclusive excerpts from our archives.

General Public Price: £15 | Subscriber Price: £10
Available from poetrylondon.co.uk

 ARTS COUNCIL
ENGLAND
Supported using public funding by

 COCHAYNE

 The London
Community
Foundation

The Poetry Society Annual Lecture Series 2021

In association with University of Liverpool

The Poetry Society and University of Liverpool's Centre for New and International Writing are delighted to present the third and final lecture in the Annual Lecture Series 2021, delivered by **m nourbeSe philip**. A poet, essayist, novelist and playwright, she is the author of the seminal *She Tries Her Tongue, Her Silence Softly Breaks* and the acclaimed book-length poem *Zong!*

m nourbeSe philip's lecture, 'Small Islands Long Poems or the (un)Epic of Small in the Spiralling Memory of History', will offer an exploration of the long poem, the poetics of the fragment and how they engage with issues of language, memory, space, place, and exile. The lecture will include a conversation between nourbeSe and Sandeep Parmar, a Q&A from the audience, and a reading of selected poems, chosen to respond to her theme.

m nourbeSe philip

Small Islands Long Poems or the (un)Epic of Small in the Spiralling Memory of History

Wednesday 3 November
7pm GMT, via ZOOM

Book online at bit.ly/annuallecturephilip

Tickets are FREE but must be reserved. Donations welcome

The Poetry Society Annual Lecture Series 2021 is presented by The Poetry Society in association with University of Liverpool (as the Kenneth Allott lectures). The first lecture in the series was given by Valzhyna Mort on 2 March 2021; Terrance Hayes delivered the second on 28 April. All three lectures are published in *The Poetry Review*.

THE**POETRY**SOCIETY

UNIVERSITY OF LIVERPOOL | Centre for New and International Writing

Supported using public funding by
ARTS COUNCIL ENGLAND

THEPOETRYSOCIETY

National Poetry Competition

Judges: Fiona Benson, David Constantine & Rachel Long

First Prize £5,000 • Second Prize £2,000 • Third Prize £1,000

Enter by 31 October 2021 at poetrysociety.org.uk/npc

ARTS COUNCIL ENGLAND

Supported using public funding by
ARTS COUNCIL
ENGLAND